HIKE THE PARKS

ACADIA NATIONAL PARK

HIKE THE PARKS

BEST DAY HIKES, WALKS, AND SIGHTS

ACADIA NATIONAL PARK

JEFFREY ROMANO

MOUNTAINEERS
BOOKS

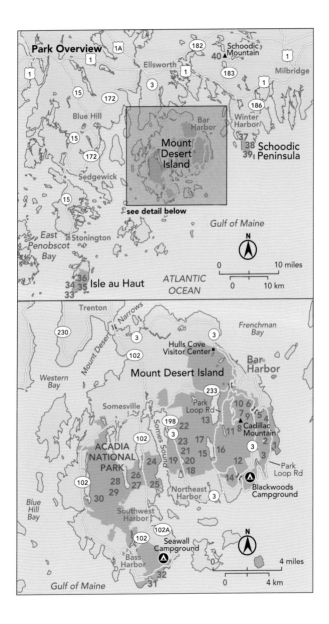

Park Overview

Ellsworth

Schoodic Mountain

Milbridge

Blue Hill

Winter Harbor

Bar Harbor

Mount Desert Island

Schoodic Peninsula

see detail below

Sedgewick

East Penobscot Bay

Stonington

Gulf of Maine

N

0 —— 10 miles

0 —— 10 km

34 35 36
33

Isle au Haut

ATLANTIC OCEAN

Trenton

Mount Desert Narrows

Frenchman Bay

Hulls Cove Visitor Center

Bar Harbor

Western Bay

Mount Desert Island

Somesville

Park Loop Rd

Somes Sound

10 6
7 9 5
8 4

Cadillac Mountain

11

3

2
1

ACADIA NATIONAL PARK

22

13

23 17
21 15 16
19 20
18

12

24

Park Loop Rd

26
28 27 25
29
30

Northeast Harbor

14

Blackwoods Campground

Blue Hill Bay

Southwest Harbor

Bass Harbor

Seawall Campground

N

0 —— 4 miles

0 —— 4 km

32
31

Gulf of Maine

HIKES AT A GLANCE

HIKE	DISTANCE miles (km)	ELEVATION GAIN feet (m)	HIGH POINT feet (m)	DIFFICULTY
FRENCHMAN BAY AND OCEAN DRIVE				
1. Great Head and Sand Beach	2 (3.2)	280 (85)	145 (44)	Easy to moderate
2. The Beehive	1.4 (2.3)	600 (185)	538 (164)	Technical
3. Gorham Mountain and Ocean Path	2.8 (4.5)	550 (170)	525 (161)	Moderate
4. Champlain Mountain and Precipice	2.7 (4.3)	1100 (335)	1063 (324)	Technical
5. Champlain Mountain and Beachcroft	2.4 (3.9)	1050 (320)	1063 (324)	Moderate to challenging
DORR AND CADILLAC MOUNTAINS				
6. Kebo Mountain	2.9 (4.7)	450 (140)	407 (124)	Moderate
7. Dorr Mountain North Ridge	3 (4.8)	1250 (380)	1270 (387)	Challenging
8. Dorr Mountain South Ridge	4.8 (7.7)	1300 (400)	1270 (387)	Challenging
9. Sieur de Monts to Jordan Pond	5.4 (8.7)	1250 (380)	990 (302)	Challenging
10. Cadillac Mountain North Ridge	5 (8)	1400 (430)	1530 (466)	Challenging
11. Cadillac Mountain West Face	4.7 (7.6)	1325 (405)	1530 (466)	Challenging
12. Cadillac Mountain South Ridge	7.4 (11.9)	1525 (465)	1530 (466)	Challenging

OPPOSITE: *Eagle Lake from atop the Bubbles Trail (Hike 13)*

HIKE	DISTANCE miles (km)	ELEVATION GAIN feet (m)	HIGH POINT feet (m)	DIFFICULTY
JORDAN POND				
13. The Bubbles and Eagle Lake	4.2 (6.8)	1000 (300)	872 (266)	Moderate to challenging
14. Day Mountain, The Triad, and Pemetic Mountain	6.8 (10.9)	1650 (505)	1248 (380)	Challenging
15. Jordan Pond Loop	3.5 (5.6)	50 (15)	300 (91)	Easy to moderate
16. Pemetic Mountain and Jordan Pond	4.2 (6.8)	1100 (335)	1248 (380)	Challenging
17. Penobscot Mountain and Jordan Cliff	4.2 (6.8)	1200 (365)	1181 (360)	Technical
NORTHEAST HARBOR				
18. Penobscot and Sargent Mountains	8 (12.9)	1750 (535)	1373 (419)	Challenging
19. Norumbega Mountain and Hadlock Ponds	3.8 (6.1)	800 (245)	846 (258)	Moderate to challenging
20. Bald Peak and Parkman Mountain	2.7 (4.3)	900 (275)	974 (297)	Moderate to challenging
21. Sargent Mountain and Hadlock Brook	4.2 (6.8)	1200 (365)	1373 (419)	Challenging
22. Sargent Mountain and Giant Slide	4.6 (7.4)	1400 (430)	1373 (419)	Challenging
23. Sargent Mountain Traverse	6.1 (9.8)	1600 (490)	1373 (419)	Challenging
SOUTHWEST HARBOR				
24. Acadia and Saint Sauveur Mountains	4.5 (7.9)	1400 (430)	690 (210)	Challenging
25. Flying Mountain	1.5 (2.4)	350 (110)	284 (87)	Easy to moderate

HIKE	DISTANCE miles (km)	ELEVATION GAIN feet (m)	HIGH POINT feet (m)	DIFFICULTY
26. Beech Cliff and Beech Mountain	3.1 (5)	900 (275)	841 (256)	Technical
27. Beech Mountain South	2.4 (3.9)	800 (245)	841 (256)	Moderate to challenging
WESTERN MOUNTAIN AND BASS HARBOR				
28. Mansell Mountain and Long Pond	4.6 (7.4)	950 (290)	949 (289)	Challenging
29. Western Mountain	3.7 (6)	1250 (380)	1071 (326)	Challenging
30. Bernard Mountain and West Ledge	3 (4.8)	1050 (320)	1071 (326)	Moderate to challenging
31. Ship Harbor Trail	1.4 (2.3)	200 (60)	50 (15)	Easy
32. Wonderland Trail	1.4 (2.3)	80 (25)	55 (17)	Easy
ISLE AU HAUT				
33. Western Head	5.8 (9.3)	600 (185)	110 (34)	Moderate to challenging
34. Ebens Head	2.7 (4.3)	150 (45)	40 (12)	Easy
35. Duck Harbor Mountain	3 (4.8)	500 (150)	308 (94)	Challenging
36. Bowditch Mountain	8.1 (13)	1050 (320)	470 (143)	Challenging
SCHOODIC PENINSULA				
37. Lower Harbor	2.1 (3.4)	200 (60)	150 (46)	Easy to moderate
38. Schoodic Head and Buck Cove Mountain	3.7 (6)	750 (230)	442 (134)	Moderate to challenging
39. Schoodic Head and The Anvil	2.5 (4)	550 (170)	442 (134)	Moderate to challenging
40. Schoodic Mountain	2.8 (4.5)	1000 (300)	1069 (326)	Challenging

VISITING ACADIA NATIONAL PARK

Regarded as the crown jewel of the North Atlantic coast, Acadia National Park features classic Maine coastal scenery, the highest mountains on America's Atlantic shores, diverse wildlife habitats, and thousands of years of human history.

Acadia has three main units. By far, the largest, oldest, and most-visited unit is spread across Mount Desert Island, which is connected to the mainland via a bridge. Acadia's most remote section is found on Isle au Haut, an area accessible by passenger ferry or private boat. Schoodic Peninsula is home to the park's only mainland unit.

Acadia encompasses more than 50,000 acres (20,200 hectares), which includes nearly 38,000 acres (15,370 hectares) of public land and more than 12,000 acres (4900 hectares) of privately owned lands, where the Park Service holds conservation easements. The easements protect the region's scenic beauty and natural resources. Stretching from the eastern edge of Penobscot Bay to the Schoodic Peninsula, Acadia displays diverse landscapes that have many natural features in common because they were shaped by similar geologic forces.

GEOLOGY

Acadia began to form more than 500 million years ago. Over the millennia that followed, volcanic eruptions, shifting

OPPOSITE: *The Beehive and Sand Beach from the Great Head Trail (Hike 1)*

continental plates, receding blocks of ice, pounding ocean surf, and harsh weather formed the bold, rocky landscape we see today.

ANCIENT LAND CARVED BY ICE

Acadia was born when mud, sand, and volcanic ash accumulated in an ocean that no longer exists. Hardened into solid bedrock through the years, the landscape eventually succumbed to the pressures of continental ice sheets.

Land of Granite. The ocean sediments that initiated Acadia's formation were buried deep under the earth's surface through the passing years. With heat and pressure, the mineral layers metamorphosed into Ellsworth Schist—a rock composed of white and gray quartz, feldspar, and green chlorite. Erosion and the movement of continental plates forced the schist to the surface. Then, roughly 450 million years ago, this oldest rock in Acadia combined with fine-grained sand and silt to create the Bar Harbor Formation. Volcanic eruptions soon contributed lava flows and ash. As the landscape cooled, Mount Desert Island's granite rocks formed. Cadillac Mountain Granite, estimated to be 420 million years old, surrounds the park's highest summit.

Years of Erosion. Not much evidence exists to capture the next few hundred million years. Softer rocks eroded, valleys formed, and harder surfaces remained. This process accelerated over the last 2 to 3 million years as successive ice ages scoured the landscape. During the most recent one, the Wisconsin glaciation, ice accumulated to a depth of 1 mile (1.6 km). This glaciation peaked around eighteen thousand years ago and lasted another six to seven thousand years.

Signs of Glaciation. Today's Acadia shows many signs of the massive ice sheet that most recently polished, scratched, and carved the mountains. Classic U-shaped valleys lie between impressive granite ridges. Scattered across the land are deposits of sand, gravel, and rock, including glacial

Bubble Rock with Eagle Lake in the distance (Hike 13)

erratics—large boulders carried as far as 20 miles (32.2 km) by the ice. Bubble Rock and many other lesser-known examples can be found throughout the park.

Changing Sea Levels. The ice sheet's size and weight also forced the land down, allowing the ocean to expand its reach. Evidence of beaches and marine caves can be found in the park, at elevations nearly 300 feet (91 m) above today's sea level. As the ice receded enough for the land to rebound and rise, glacial deposits formed dams that cut off salt water to low-lying areas. Today, these basins are home to many of the region's freshwater lakes and ponds.

ACADIA TODAY

When the glaciers finally disappeared more than eleven thousand years ago, they left behind a landscape dominated by three natural features.

Rocky Shoreline. Surrounded by the cold waters of the Gulf of Maine, Acadia is home to more than 40 miles (64 km) of rocky shoreline highlighted with scenic promontories, steep

15

cliffs, narrow chasms, and smooth ledges. Hidden within the coves, inlets, and peninsulas are many beaches. Due to the age of the coast, cobble beaches are more common than sandy ones. Not the best places for a swim, these rocky beaches generate an alluring sound as the waves roll in and out with the tides.

Expansive Wetlands. Wetland habitats make up more than 20 percent of Acadia. These include marshes and estuaries where fresh water and salt water collide. Acadia is also home to many small streams, brooks, bogs, vernal pools, and forested wetlands. In addition, there are fourteen lakes and ponds greater than 10 acres (4 hectares) as well as ten ponds smaller in size either within or adjacent to the park. Collectively, Acadia's wetlands are critically important to the region's flora and fauna, and many provide fresh drinking water to local communities.

Coastal Mountains. Compared to many mountain ranges around the world, Acadia's peaks are merely hills rising to only 1530 feet (466 m). Yet their proximity to the ocean, the ruggedness of their slopes, and their miles of exposed granite combine to transform these diminutive heights into impressive summits and breathtakingly beautiful mountains. The park's topography exhibits significant differences across modest elevation changes; plant and animal species vary with the ascent, as do weather conditions, which can change quickly. There are no other places like Acadia's mountains along America's Atlantic coast.

EVOLVING LANDSCAPE

In the wake of the most recent ice age, changes to Acadia's landscape have been slow and subtle. Each year, running water polishes the granite surfaces, winter's expanding ice separates rocks from mountainsides, waves shape the ledge-covered shoreline, and storms move smaller debris to shift the park's beaches. While the landscape continues to

FIRES OF 1947

In mid-October 1947, after a hot, dry summer and fall, wildfires broke out on Mount Desert Island. Ten days later they were under control, but not until more than 17,000 acres (6900 hectares), 170 homes, and 5 historic hotels had burned. Not an isolated event, fires claimed an additional 180,000 acres (73,000 hectares) in other parts of Maine that year. While devastating at the time, Acadia's forest today is healthier and more diverse as a result—benefiting natural beauty and wildlife.

evolve slowly, human activities are accelerating many natural processes as the changing climate increases average temperatures, sea level rise, and storm intensities.

FLORA AND FAUNA

Acadia has a broad array of flora and fauna. The park's plant and animal diversity can be attributed to its mountainous topography, abundant wetlands, geographic location, and climate.

FORESTS ON THE EDGE

Much like the rest of Maine, most of Acadia is forested. Which trees grow where depends on many factors, including elevation, slope direction, fire history, and soil qualities. The park also sits on the boundary between two major ecoregions: the southern edge of the boreal forest that extends into Canada and the northern edge of the eastern deciduous forest that stretches south toward the mid-Atlantic.

Boreal Forests. Large portions of the park are home to red spruce, white spruce, and balsam fir. These boreal species are prevalent along the shoreline, across Isle au Haut, throughout the Schoodic Peninsula, and on the higher elevations of Mount Desert Island where soils are thin. Northern white cedar, a less widespread boreal species, lines the shores of many of the park's ponds and lakes. While dominated by evergreens, the park's boreal forests are also home to a scattering of hardwood trees.

Eastern Deciduous. Eastern deciduous trees thrive in lower elevations away from the ocean, along south-facing slopes where soils are healthier, and in areas impacted by fire. Common species include eastern beech, white and yellow birch, red and sugar maple, white ash, and red oak. These are the trees whose leaves change, creating a palette of colors across the landscape before falling to the ground each autumn. In some locations, these deciduous trees grow in mixed stands with white pines, the region's tallest conifer.

Isolated Forests. Acadia also features a handful of smaller forest communities, including pitch pine, scrub oak, and jack pine woodlands. These forests generally grow on ledge-covered, higher-elevation terrain with thin soils and persistent winds. Many of the pitch and jack pines thrive on summits and ridges that were significantly impacted by the infamous 1947 fire (see "Fires of 1947" sidebar). Look for stands of eastern hemlock growing along streambeds at lower elevations in the mountains.

CARPETS OF PLANTS AND FUNGI

The combination of Acadia's mountains and its proximity to the ocean leads to a summer climate that is moister and cooler than that of flatter, nearby inland regions. Often shrouded in fog, especially early in the summer, the park is fertile ground for more than a thousand species of plants and fungi.

Wildflowers. On most hikes in the park, you will encounter many different species of wildflowers. In the forests, look for carpets of bunchberry and bluebead lily as well as many other less showy and less common species. Rhodora and sheep laurel add color and texture to the park's rocky

Rhodora adds splashes of bright color to Acadia in late spring.

summits and open areas at different times throughout the spring and summer. During the fall, the bright red leaves of highbush blueberry do the same, along with the purple petals of asters.

Wetland Plants. Acadia's freshwater wetlands provide fertile grounds, home to roughly eighty plants. Some of the most sensitive wetland species are found in the region's bogs, where sphagnum moss, pitcher plants, and Labrador tea find ways to thrive. The park is also home to many intertidal marine plants and algae, including rockweed, that provide critical habitat for many wildlife species during low and high tides.

Ferns, Mosses, and Fungi. The park's cool, wet climate sustains many species of ferns, mosses, and fungi, which thrive in shady, wet soils. The ferns, surfacing in the spring, add greenery well into the fall. Mushrooms and other fungi are most abundant in the late summer and early autumn. Picking mushrooms is prohibited in the park, but marveling at their many shapes and colors is not.

Grasses. By far the most common plants encountered in the park are "grasses." Approximately one in four Acadia plants fall into this category, which includes grasses, sedges, and rushes. Atop the park's mountain ridges many of these species are fragile. Be sure to stay on trails and rocky surfaces to avoid trampling these high-elevation plants.

Non-Native Species. In the four centuries following the arrival of European settlers to the region, Acadia's plant composition has changed a great deal. Today, nearly 25 percent of all plant species in the park are non-native. Among the non-native plants, roughly thirty species significantly harm native plants and habitats. Acadia park management continues to find ways to minimize the impacts of these exotic plants.

WILDLIFE ABOUNDS

You never know what you will spot around the next bend. Acadia's habitat diversity is home to approximately 40 species of mammals, more than 330 species of birds, 30 species of fish, 7 reptiles, and 11 amphibians. Although their extent is less well known, the park's most common wildlife species are invertebrates—some that can be a nuisance and many that are critical components of the food web. Here are some species you may encounter.

ACADIA BIRDING FESTIVAL

An annual event that began in the late 1990s, the Acadia Birding Festival welcomes avian enthusiasts to Mount Desert Island during the peak of spring migration. The multiday event takes place in late May or early June. This is one of the quieter times of the year to visit Acadia and the best season to enjoy the region's diversity of bird species. Registration is limited, so reserve your spot well in advance. Expert guides lead tours in the park, to nearby lands, and across surrounding waters.

Red squirrels forage near many Acadia trails.

Mammals. Since most mammals avoid human beings, they can be difficult to spot. Red squirrels are probably the most visible furry creatures. Among the park's larger mammals, white-tailed deer are the least reclusive—look for them feeding in open areas. If you spend enough time in Acadia, with a little luck you may also cross paths with porcupines, foxes, mink, otters, fishers, martens, bobcats, beavers, raccoons, bats, coyotes, snowshoe hares, and even an occasional black bear or moose. In addition, marine mammals such as harbor seals and porpoises can be spotted from many of the coastal trails.

Birds. Acadia is considered one of the best birdwatching destinations in the country (see "Acadia Birding Festival" sidebar). More than 330 avian species have been recorded in the park. In the spring, Acadia welcomes the arrival of dozens of colorful songbirds—some nest in the park, but many continue north. Raptors, including nesting peregrine falcons, wintering snowy owls, majestic bald eagles, and migrating hawks in the fall, are a big draw for birders. The park's marine habitat lures sea ducks, great blue herons, sandpipers, belted kingfishers, and loons. While exploring Acadia's forested trails, listen for woodpeckers, thrushes, vireos, kinglets, and warblers. Atop rocky summits spot juncos

Black-throated green warblers nest throughout the park.

and white-throated sparrows and the soaring wings of turkey vultures. Every season is different, but Acadia offers bird-watching opportunities twelve months a year.

Amphibians and Reptiles. Despite the park's harsh winter weather, eleven species of amphibians and seven species of reptiles call Acadia home. You will encounter American toads more than other amphibians, but five species of frogs and five species of salamanders live in the park as well. As winter temperatures fade, listen for spring peepers on warm evenings and wood frogs in vernal pools. Acadia's reptiles are mostly secretive. However, you will often spot docile garter snakes seeking the sun's warm rays in open areas; painted turtles do the same on pond logs and rocks. None of the five resident snake species are poisonous. Similarly, despite their appearance, snapping turtles pose no danger to humans— just give them ample space when they are seeking sandy places to lay eggs in early summer.

VIEWING WILDLIFE

Generally, early morning and late afternoon are the best times to spot wildlife, but minimizing noise is always helpful.

When encountering wildlife, enjoy from a distance (binoculars work well), please don't feed the wildlife (it will only hurt their future survivability), and make sure your dog is leashed (wildlife have enough challenges already). The Park Service recommends remaining 50 feet (about one bus length) from birds, reptiles, and small mammals, 150 feet from seals, and 100 feet from deer, foxes, and other large mammals. In addition to adhering to these distance recommendations, please view animals from the trail rather than trampling vegetation to get a better look.

ACADIA HISTORY

Because Acadia was the first national park established in the eastern United States, it has been influenced by humans more than most. This human history has shaped the park and is as much a part of it as are the natural forces. Acadia's history is one of revering, discovering, enjoying, and conserving the region's scenic beauty and vast ecological resources.

PEOPLE OF THE DAWNLAND

Native Americans were the first people to call this land their home, arriving in Maine roughly twelve thousand years ago.

ABBE MUSEUM

Visit the Abbe Museum to learn more about the People of the Dawnland, the Wabanaki, who were the first to call Acadia their home. The museum has two locations: a main building in downtown Bar Harbor that is open year-round and the original location at Sieur de Monts Spring that is open during the summer. Check out their website for the most up-to-date schedule and to learn about upcoming exhibits and programming (see Contact Information).

Through the centuries these initial inhabitants of the region divided into four nations: the Maliseet, Mi'kmaq, Passamaquoddy, and Penobscot. Together they are called the Wabanaki, which means "People of the Dawnland." For centuries prior to the arrival of European explorers, the Wabanaki gathered food, raised families, and flourished on and around Mount Desert Island as well as throughout the area now known as Maine. Using birchbark canoes, they were able to travel the surrounding coastal waters to conduct trade and gather staples for life. At the same time, the Wabanaki formed a special, spiritual connection to this land—its mountains, the rising sun, the rivers and waters, and the rocky shoreline.

L'ÎLE DES MONTS DÉSERTS

Some believe Norse Vikings visited Maine around the twelfth century. Italian sailor Giovanni da Verrazzano ventured along the New England coast in 1524. However, it was not until 1604 that French explorer and cartographer Samuel de Champlain first wrote about the land that is now Acadia National Park. He called the largest island "L'île des Monts Déserts" or "the Island of Barren Mountains." Today, it is called Mount Desert (pronounced *dessert*) Island. Champlain also named many other natural features in the area, including nearby Isle au Haut or "High Island."

The French settlers were also responsible for the park's name. In the early seventeenth century, the word Acadia was used by fishermen and traders to describe an area encompassing portions of New England and the Canadian Maritimes. Some historians believe the term comes from a Mi'kmaq word meaning "piece of land."

By 1613, French Jesuits had established a mission on Mount Desert Island, their first in North America. But, shortly after being established, the mission was destroyed by the English, effectively ending French influence in the region.

BRITISH AND AMERICAN SETTLEMENT

Mount Desert Island was largely ignored by French and English settlers over the next 150 years, with the French focusing their interests in Canada and the English focusing on the region around Boston. However, with the British victory in the French and Indian War, boundary disputes between the two European powers ended in 1763. English settlers soon began to arrive in the area. After the Revolutionary War, even more people came in search of farmland, forest products, and jobs in a growing shipbuilding industry.

RUSTICATORS AND ARTISTS

In the mid-1800s, Mount Desert Island transformed, becoming a growing haven for so-called rusticators: wealthy families in search of summer retreats, inspired by painters and writers who had captured the region's beauty. By the 1880s, a time of significant economic growth in the United States, some of the country's most noteworthy and successful business leaders had established permanent summer "cottages" on the island. The Rockefellers, Morgans, Fords, Vanderbilts, Carnegies, and Astors were some of the notable families who built large estates in this era.

CONSERVING ACADIA

As Mount Desert Island's popularity increased, public access to the region's mountains, forests, and shoreline became more tenuous. In response, a growing number of people saw land conservation as necessary to protect the area's heritage. They worked to find a balance between development and public access to the island's spectacular natural features.

The Eliots. As the turn of the twentieth century approached, Charles Eliot, a summer resident, grew concerned that private ownership could mean the end of public access to the region's unique natural features. He saw this potential as a loss not only to the state's heritage but also to its future prosperity. Charles died at the young age of thirty-eight in 1897, but his father Charles W. Eliot was inspired by his son's writings. In 1901, he led the effort to establish the Hancock County Trustees of Reservation.

Hancock County Trustees of Reservation. This conservation organization grew naturally out of a movement that began in the 1880s when summer residents formed village improvement associations focused on sanitation, community gatherings, and the construction of hiking trails. The next step was "acquiring, owning and holding lands and other property in Hancock County for free public use." This was Maine's conservation movement in its infancy.

George B. Dorr. Not surprisingly, the effort to preserve land on Mount Desert Island took time and faced roadblocks. Landowners were skeptical of selling or donating their properties. Town officials raised concerns about property tax losses. George B. Dorr emerged as the most vocal land conservation champion. He effectively made the case for land protection at the local, state, and federal levels. This mission would consume the final forty-three years of his life.

Sieur de Monts National Monument. Thanks to the leadership of the Eliots, George Dorr, and others, by 1913 the Hancock County Trustees of Reservation had acquired more than 5000 acres (2000 hectares). Dorr traveled to Washington, DC, and offered this land to the federal government, and in 1916, President Woodrow Wilson accepted the land, declaring it Sieur de Monts National Monument.

ESTABLISHING A NATIONAL PARK

The American National Park System began in 1872 with the creation of Yellowstone National Park. In the four decades that followed, Congress established parks throughout the western United States, each time from lands with only one owner in the chain of title: the federal government. George Dorr and his Hancock County Trustees of Reservation allies had the idea to establish the first national park in the eastern United States.

Lafayette National Park. After the 1916 creation of Sieur de Monts National Monument, Dorr continued to acquire lands on Mount Desert Island as he lobbied to transform the property into a national park. Both designations ensure long-term land protection, but national park status, which requires an act of Congress, is limited to those areas that "possess nationally significant natural, cultural, or recreational resources." In 1919, Dorr's persistence and determination succeeded. President Wilson signed into law an act to establish Lafayette National Park, the first of its kind east of the Mississippi River. The name was proposed during World War I, when the United States backed France, to honor a famous French officer who had served with George Washington during the Revolutionary War. Soon after, George Dorr was hired as the park's first superintendent.

KEY STATS: ACADIA NATIONAL PARK

- Established 1916 as Sieur de Monts National Monument; 1919 as Lafayette National Park; 1929 as Acadia National Park
- Average annual visitation: Approximately 3.5 million
- Acreage: More than 50,000 acres (20,200 hectares), which includes nearly 38,000 acres (15,370 hectares) of public land and 12,000 acres (4900 hectares) of conservation easements
- Sections: Mount Desert Island, Schoodic, and Isle au Haut
- Campgrounds: Blackwoods, Seawall, Schoodic Woods, and Duck Harbor
- Total hiking trails: 158 miles (254 km)
- Historic carriage roads: 45 miles (72 km)
- High point: 1530 feet (466 m; Cadillac Mountain)
- Low point: Sea level (multiple locations)

Acadia Forms and Grows. In the late 1920s, John Moore of Steuben left his property on the Schoodic Peninsula to his daughters in England. They wanted to donate their family land to the park, but as British citizens they had reservations about honoring Lafayette. In 1929, Congress accepted the Schoodic land donation and changed the park's name to Acadia, a term that more accurately captured the region's history. Acadia has continued to slowly grow larger over the years. In 1943, a generous landowner donated roughly half of Isle au Haut to the park. Throughout much of the twentieth century new parcels were added to the Mount Desert Island section as the park expanded west from Bar Harbor to include lands on both sides of Somes Sound.

Boundary Finalized. The present park boundary is largely the result of legislation passed by Congress in 1986. Within the boundary today, private lands exist. These are the only properties Acadia can add to the park without further congressional authority. Thanks to financial support from the Land and Water Conservation Fund established by Congress in 1964 and from private philanthropy, Acadia has purchased many private inholdings within its boundary in recent decades. This effort continues today.

Conservation Easements. On the periphery of the 1986 boundary, the park is also authorized to hold conservation easements on private lands. These voluntary agreements enhance the park by permanently protecting scenic values and natural resources. Acadia holds easements on more than 12,000 acres (4900 hectares) in the region.

Schoodic Expands. In 2019, Congress expanded the 1986 border when it accepted the donation of 1440 acres (600 hectares) on the Schoodic Peninsula. With this donation, the park grew to more than 50,000 acres (20,200 hectares) of land across the Mount Desert Island archipelago from Isle au Haut to the Schoodic Peninsula.

MAINE COAST HERITAGE TRUST

Maine Coast Heritage Trust (MCHT) conserves and stewards Maine's coastal lands and islands for their renowned scenic beauty, ecological value, outdoor recreational opportunities, and contribution to community well-being. Building on Acadia's proud tradition of land conservation, the trust began in 1970 to help the park add land and acquire conservation easements. Supported by members, MCHT is now a statewide land trust that invites the public to explore its network of preserves from Casco Bay to Eastport, including many properties in the Acadia region.

TRAILS OF ACADIA

The final piece of the Acadia puzzle has been the development of recreational infrastructure so that visitors can safely explore and enjoy the park's natural splendor. At the heart of Acadia's recreational opportunities is its network of trails: more than 150 miles (241 km) of hiking trails, 45 miles (72 km) of carriage roads, and 8 miles (12.9 km) of bicycle paths.

Hiking Trails. Most of the hiking trails that wind around Mount Desert Island were established in the 1890s when village improvement associations laid out and constructed many of them. In 1896, Waldron Bates was the lead author of the island's first hiking map, which closely resembles today's version.

A trail pioneer, Bates also designed the area's first trail construction and maintenance handbook. Thanks to Bates, there are few hiking trails in New England that exhibit the same level of artistry, erosion control, and assistance for scaling steep inclines as those that traverse Acadia National Park. He is also credited with the creation of the park's unique cairn style.

Carriage Roads. Acadia's network of carriage roads showcases a bygone era in the United States. Separate from the

FRIENDS OF ACADIA

Friends of Acadia (FOA) preserves, protects, and promotes stewardship of the outstanding natural beauty, ecological vitality, and distinctive cultural resources of Acadia National Park and surrounding communities for the inspiration and enjoyment of current and future generations. The nonprofit membership organization works with the park to identify places and projects where its members' expertise and assistance can most benefit Acadia's critical needs. FOA works on the park's hiking trails, supports the Island Explorer bus service, and maintains other programs to enhance visitor experiences.

park's automobile roads, this 45-mile (72-km) recreational network combines artistic beauty with a design that facilitates a deliberate and leisurely paced exploration of the park by foot, bike, or horseback.

The carriage roads were financially supported by John D. Rockefeller Jr. Through his leadership, the roads became more than a way to get from here to there. Constructed between 1913 and 1940, the carriage roads feature a system of seventeen stone-faced bridges and a handful of gatehouses. The stone-faced bridges were designed to fit the surrounding landscape by complementing each location's unique stream and geology.

Rockefeller worked with landscape architect Beatrix Farrand to ensure the carriage roads were lined with native trees, shrubs, and plants—sixty varieties were planted along the corridors. Farrand designed the plantings to feel seamless, as if the new flora had existed before the roads were constructed.

Biking Paths. The latest addition to Acadia's trail network is more than 8 miles (12.9 km) of bicycle paths on the Schoodic

Peninsula. This network has a similar feel to the carriage roads of Mount Desert Island, but with a less elaborate design. The trails are used by bikers and hikers to enjoy this quieter corner of the park.

MUST-SEE SIGHTS AND ACTIVITIES

The Acadia region boasts a wide array of outdoor activities and must-see destinations. Every visitor should consider these quintessential activities. You won't be alone on many, but you will quickly understand why.

PARK LOOP ROAD'S OCEAN DRIVE

Brave the cold waters at Sand Beach, watch the tide roll in at Thunder Hole as it crashes in the narrow shoreline chasm, snap a photo of Otter Cliff, and enjoy the company.

CADILLAC MOUNTAIN

Head to the highest point on America's eastern seaboard for sweeping mountain views or leave the crowds behind by scaling Sargent Mountain's slightly lower (but more scenic) summit.

SCHOODIC POINT

Marvel at the waves pounding Schoodic Point's granite shoreline, a dream location from sunrise to sunset for painters and photographers.

FRENCHMAN BAY PADDLE

Launch a kayak into Frenchman Bay to enjoy a different perspective of Mount Desert Island's mountains and rocky coast.

BUBBLE ROCK

Hike to Bubble Rock for a bird's-eye view of Jordan Pond and a panorama of higher peaks in most directions.

Bass Harbor Head Lighthouse, a popular place to capture sunsets

BASS HARBOR HEAD LIGHTHOUSE

Snap a photograph of the Bass Harbor Head Lighthouse, perched high atop a coastal bluff, with the islands of Blue Hill Bay dotting the horizon.

LADDER TRAILS

Enjoy intimate cliffside views by scaling one of the park's ladder trails: Jordan Cliff, the Beehive, Dorr Ladder, the Precipice, or Beech Cliff.

JORDAN POND HOUSE

Step back in time at the Jordan Pond House by dining on popovers, sipping tea, enjoying the well-manicured landscape, and gazing out across the sparkling waters.

CARRIAGE ROADS

Tour the carriage roads by bike or horseback from late spring through fall or head out on cross-country skis or snowshoes in the heart of winter.

CLIFF TRAIL

Explore Western Head and the Cliff Trail on Isle au Haut to partake of coastal scenery more dramatic and wilder than Ocean Drive—and far less crowded!

WHALE WATCH

Head out on a whale-watching tour for the chance to see marine mammals and pelagic birds; in early summer, be sure your tour swings by the puffin colony on Petit Manan Island.

LOBSTER DINNER

Enjoy a classic Maine lobster dinner with Maine potatoes, corn, and blueberry pie. There are countless restaurants to choose from in nearby communities and many local brews to pair with your meal.

PLANNING YOUR TRIP

Before heading to Acadia for your next hiking adventure, it is critical to do some research in advance. The following is a good starting point, but check the park's website for the latest information.

VISITOR CENTERS

Located just off Route 3 north of Bar Harbor and at the northern entrance to Park Loop Road, **Hulls Cove** is Acadia's main visitor center. Visitors can purchase an entrance pass, speak with a ranger, view local art, use self-service maps, purchase merchandise, and gather information. Park here to access Island Explorer buses, which run seasonally from late June to mid-October. This visitor center is typically closed late fall through early spring but check the park website to confirm hours of operation.

Acadia has a handful of additional smaller visitor centers scattered across Mount Desert Island. Basic park information, park passes, and Island Explorer buses can be accessed at the **Village Green Information Center**. Located on Firefly Lane, it sits on the northern side of the Bar Harbor Village Green. South of Bar Harbor, near the intersection of Route 3 and Park Loop Road, find the **Sieur de Monts Nature Center**, where you can look at exhibits, gather park and hiking trail information, and tour the Wild Gardens of Acadia—an outdoor collection of native plants found in the park.

OPPOSITE: *Otter Point, veiled in fog, from the Gorham Mountain Trail (Hike 3)*

Two visitor centers are available on the Schoodic Peninsula. At the **Schoodic Woods Ranger Station**, you can gather park information, purchase a park pass, and access Island Explorer buses in season. Near Schoodic Point, find the **Rockefeller Welcome Center**, home to exhibits describing the former navy base that now houses it.

Most travelers to Isle au Haut arrive in Duck Harbor. Although Duck Harbor has no visitor center, a park ranger generally awaits new arrivals. In addition, a small **Isle au Haut Ranger Station** is on Main Road about 0.5 mile (0.8 km) south of the Isle au Haut Town Landing. This is also the northern terminus of the Duck Harbor Trail.

In an effort to relieve traffic congestion, Acadia National Park is working with state and local partners to develop a new visitor center at the Acadia Gateway Center in Trenton. Conveniently located just off Route 3, minutes north of Mount Desert Island, the new facility will include parking, a small store, an information desk where visitors can purchase park passes, and a hub where visitors can hop on Island Explorer buses to access the park. Construction is scheduled be completed as early as 2022.

CAMPING

Acadia National Park offers camping at four diverse sites. Camping within the park is limited to these destinations and one other that is not run by the park and is for equestrians and stock animals. Backcountry camping, sleeping in your car, or parking your trailer outside a campground are prohibited. There are also many nearby private campgrounds.

Of the four campgrounds run by the park, Duck Harbor offers the most basic services. In addition to its five lean-to sites, it has composting toilets, drinking water, and picnic tables. Blackwoods, Seawall, and Schoodic, with sites that accommodate RVs and tents, provide visitors with flush toilets, running water, and picnic tables.

MOUNT DESERT ISLAND

Three campgrounds are found on Mount Desert Island. **Blackwoods Campground** (281 sites) on Route 3 south of Bar Harbor is the park's largest and the closest camping option to Acadia's most-visited destinations and most-popular hiking trails. On the quieter side of the island, just 4 miles (6.4 km) from Southwest Harbor, you will find **Seawall Campground** (201 sites). Although not run by the park, **Wildwood Stables Campground**, a third campground within Acadia, is available to visitors with stock animals.

SCHOODIC PENINSULA AND ISLE AU HAUT

The Schoodic Peninsula and Isle au Haut sections of the park each offer one camping option. Acadia's newest campground is **Schoodic Woods** (89 sites), conveniently located near the start of the peninsula's scenic loop road. On Isle au Haut, small lean-tos shelter overnight guests at the park's most remote campground, **Duck Harbor** (5 sites). Although Duck Harbor is not accessible by road, during the operating season daily private passenger-only boat service is available from Stonington to the campground.

RESERVING A CAMPSITE

Opening and closing dates for Acadia's campgrounds vary, although all open in the spring and close in the fall. The Park Service recommends making reservations before your arrival and requires reservations at **Duck Harbor**. Depending on the campground and time of year, reservations well in advance are necessary because sites fill up quickly. Visit the park website for information on rates, reservations, availability of

The gateway to Isle au Haut, Stonington is home to Maine's highest annual lobster landings.

group sites, and dates of operation. Reservations at Duck Harbor often fill within minutes of opening, so be sure to plan well in advance.

GATEWAY TOWNS

Acadia is surrounded by many communities that offer lodging, dining, and other services for park visitors.

BAR HARBOR

Acadia's original gateway community, Bar Harbor has attracted visitors for more than a century. Its classic New England Village Green is surrounded by a network of roads with inns, restaurants, shops, groceries, and other businesses. Located on Frenchman Bay, Bar Harbor also has a commercial waterfront with whale-watching boats, sightseeing cruises, and kayak rentals. The town is close to the park's most-popular destinations.

MOUNT DESERT, SOUTHWEST HARBOR, AND TREMONT

Located on both sides of Somes Sound and west to Blue Hill Bay, these three communities on Mount Desert Island provide quieter destinations than Bar Harbor. All three offer convenient access to Acadia's main attractions but are closer to less-traveled sites. Visitors will find a wide selection of accommodations, dining experiences, and other services.

ELLSWORTH

The largest city in Hancock County, Ellsworth has everything a traveler would need, from overnight rooms and restaurants to groceries and supplies. With normal traffic, the city is located about a half hour from the Hulls Cove Visitor Center and about forty-five minutes from the Schoodic Woods Campground.

WINTER HARBOR AND GOULDSBORO

The Schoodic Peninsula lies south of the small coastal villages of Winter Harbor and Gouldsboro. While these two municipalities offer fewer services than the gateway communities on Mount Desert Island, they welcome travelers looking for a more relaxed adventure. B&Bs, restaurants, small stores, and other businesses offer services to visitors.

DEER ISLE AND STONINGTON

Find the communities of Deer Isle and Stonington at the southern end of Route 15. The heart of Maine's lobster industry, Stonington is a working waterfront. Along its narrow streets are small inns, quaint shops, and quality local foods. Grab the passenger-only ferry to Isle au Haut in Stonington, a good place to stock up before your journey.

GETTING AROUND

While Acadia was designed with the automobile in mind, current traffic patterns differ significantly from the 1930s. In response, Acadia National Park and private partners, including Friends of Acadia and L.L. Bean, have developed a free, user-friendly Island Explorer bus service that provides convenient transportation to the most-popular destinations during the busiest times of the year. More-energetic visitors can also take advantage of bike-friendly options.

DRIVING TO TRAILHEADS

All of Acadia's trailheads on Mount Desert Island and the Schoodic Peninsula are accessible by private vehicle. Schoodic Peninsula is served entirely by a Park Service road. Access to trails on Mount Desert Island is provided by a combination of Park Service roads, state highways, and other public rights-of-way. There are seasonal closures on some of the park's roads and limits on parking spaces. Visit Acadia's website for up-to-date regulations and information.

Park Loop Road. Providing access to the heart of Acadia's Mount Desert Island section, the scenic 27-mile (43-km) Park Loop Road starts at the Hulls Cove Visitor Center and visits the park's most-popular hiking destinations. It includes **Cadillac Summit Road**, where RVs and trailers are prohibited. Significant portions of the loop road are one-way traffic only in a clockwise direction. The multiple entrances include its intersections with Route 233, Route 3, Otter Cliff Road, and Stanley Brook Road. An entrance station is located 1 mile (1.6 km) north of Sand Beach. The busiest section of Park Loop Road is from Sand Beach to Otter Point, which is also referred to as **Ocean Drive**. Follow all parking regulations at trailheads. If parking is allowed on the road itself (allowed on some sections of the one-way portion), park in the right-hand lane on the pavement.

Network of Paved and Unpaved Roads. On the western side of Mount Desert Island, Acadia maintains numerous paved and unpaved roads that provide access to hiking trailheads near Echo Lake, Beech Mountain, and Western Mountain. These trailheads also have limited parking, which is mostly an issue near Beech Mountain.

State Highways and Public Roads. Many trailheads on Mount Desert Island are located on state highways and public roads, including Routes 3/198 near Northeast Harbor, Route 102 between Somesville and Southwest Harbor, and Route 102A near Bass Harbor. These trailheads are accessible year-round, although the parking areas may not be plowed in winter. While parking is generally allowed on the sides of these public roads, be sure not to impede or interfere with traffic.

Schoodic Loop Road. Schoodic Loop Road provides access to the scenic peninsula. The entrance is located on Route 186, just east of Winter Harbor's village center. It leads south, providing two-way traffic to just beyond Schoodic Woods Campground. Beyond the campground, RVs and trailers are prohibited. At the Frazer Point Picnic Area, a 6-mile (10-km), one-way loop begins. Stopping on the road and parking outside of designated pullouts are prohibited. Near the tip of the peninsula, a two-way spur leads to rocky Schoodic Point. A public road connects the eastern end of the one-way loop with Route 186 in Birch Harbor.

USING THE ISLAND EXPLORER BUSES

In the summer and fall, Park Loop Road, popular trailheads, and parking lots at carriage road entrances can be quite busy. To avoid crowds, slow traffic, and full parking lots, head to the trailhead in the comfort and convenience of a fare-free Island Explorer bus. Buses run from late June through mid-October, providing service between park destinations, local communities, and the Bar Harbor–Hancock County Regional Airport. The buses run throughout the day and stop at campgrounds, carriage road entrances, and many trailheads. You can also flag down buses or ask the driver to make a special stop along any of the routes. Drivers will pick up or drop off passengers anywhere it is safe to do so. Bus schedules are available at a variety of locations including visitor centers, campgrounds, and on the Island Explorer website.

A SAFER AND MORE EFFICIENT TRANSPORTATION PLAN

The Park Service released a transportation plan in 2019 to "outline a comprehensive approach to providing safe and efficient transportation to visitors to Acadia National Park while ensuring that park resources and values are protected and visitors are able to enjoy a variety of high-quality experiences." The plan was developed with years of research, data gathering, public input, and analysis. Following are some of the highlights of changes scheduled to occur in the years to come.

Timed-Entry Reservations. The Park Service will operate a timed-entry reservation system for the most-popular sections of Park Loop Road, including the Jordan Pond parking lot, Cadillac Summit Road, and the Ocean Drive corridor. To access these portions of the road in a private vehicle, visitors will need to reserve a time window in which to enter but are not required to exit by a particular time. The initial plan is to implement this reservation system for the high season, between mid-June and mid-October, but this timeline may change in response to actual demand. Once you are on Ocean Drive, all parking lots will continue to be available on a first-come, first-served basis. In other words, a reservation allowing access to Ocean Drive will not guarantee a parking spot at your desired trailhead. In addition, the Park Service will be working toward eliminating right-lane parking, currently allowed at the Precipice Trail and along Ocean Drive. Those wishing to bypass the reservation system to access Ocean Drive or Jordan Pond can use the reservation-free, fare-free Island Explorer bus service. The Island Explorer does not service Cadillac Summit Road.

Parking Lot and Island Explorer Expansion. To facilitate the implementation of the reservation system and address other parking issues, Acadia plans to redesign and expand parking lots at Jordan Pond, Eagle Lake, and the Hulls Cove Visitor Center. At Hulls Cove, they hope to nearly double the 270 parking spaces to around 500. Changes to the Hulls Cove Visitor Center will complement an effort to improve the Acadia Gateway Center, a regional transportation hub in the town of Trenton. The Acadia Gateway Center is on Route 3, just a few minutes north of the bridge crossing to Mount Desert Island. These two changes will be part of a larger effort to improve and expand the Island Explorer bus service. Enhancing this free public transportation system will ensure this service continues to be an attractive alternative to driving a vehicle in the park.

BIKING

Take a break from hiking to explore Mount Desert Island's multiuse carriage roads, Schoodic Peninsula's bike trails, or Isle au Haut's lightly traveled paved and unpaved roads by bicycle. Similarly, all three destinations can be enjoyed through combination "hike and bike" adventures. On Mount Desert Island and Schoodic, seasonal Island Explorer buses will transport your bikes with you. The Isle au Haut ferry will get your bike to the island for a small fee. Bikes can be offloaded only at the Isle au Haut Town Landing, not at Duck Harbor. Bring your own bike or find a local outfitter near any of the three Acadia destinations—it is a great way to see the park at a slower pace. If you plan on biking Park Loop Road, consider completing your ride before vehicle traffic picks up around 9:00 AM. The lack of a bike lane, parked cars, and narrow corridors make sticking to carriage roads a safer option by midmorning.

ISLE AU HAUT FERRY

The most convenient way to access Isle au Haut is via the Isle au Haut Boat Services Mail Boat out of Stonington, which provides service to the island for passengers and bicycles. The boat stops at the Isle au Haut Town Landing on the north end of the island and Duck Harbor to the south, with more frequent and year-round stops to the town landing. Acadia's trails are accessible from either stop, but Duck Harbor is more convenient for reaching the campground and the park's most scenic hikes. It is possible to arrive at the Isle au Haut Town Landing and depart at Duck Harbor, or vice versa. Arriving and departing Duck Harbor on the same day allows for at least a few hours of exploration on the island. The ferry traverses mostly protected waters to and from the island, offering pleasant scenery and wildlife viewing opportunities. Dogs are not allowed at Duck Harbor Campground but are permitted on

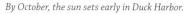
By October, the sun sets early in Duck Harbor.

the ferry for those visiting for the day. Visit the Isle au Haut Boat Services website for the latest schedule, information, and rates (see Contact Information). Although no car ferries serve Isle au Haut, there are cars on the island—barged there by residents and property owners. Island traffic is light.

WHEN TO VISIT

Hikers can explore Acadia year-round, but most visitors arrive from late June to mid-October. Trails are less crowded between late October and mid-June and in September (fall foliage draws many visitors during the first few weeks of October).

Most trails and amenities are open to the public from mid-April through October. However, the Park Service may close roads, facilities, and trails at any time to protect wildlife, respond to weather incidents, address safety concerns, or for maintenance. Check the park's website for the latest information on closures.

SEASONAL WILDLIFE-RELATED CLOSURES

Hikers should be aware that in most years, the Precipice, Jordan Cliff, part of the Orange and Black, and Valley Cove Trails are closed from spring to midsummer because of nesting peregrine falcons. These trails do not open until the young have fledged, which is usually around early August.

WEATHER AND CLIMATE

Acadia has a wet climate with significant weather changes, month to month and day to day. Just south of the forty-fifth parallel, the park has four distinct seasons. However, due to its coastal proximity, weather extremes are slightly more moderate than at nearby inland locations: Acadia's spring weather generally begins sooner, summer days are often cooler, fall conditions arrive later, and winter temperatures remain milder.

A CHANGING CLIMATE

Earth's climate has been changing more rapidly in recent years, which scientists attribute largely to human activities that have increased atmospheric carbon dioxide and other greenhouse gases. Based on current data and computer projections, Acadia will likely experience higher seas and stronger storm surges, more intense precipitation events, warmer and more acidic ocean water, and milder year-round temperatures. Flora and fauna are also likely to change as southern species expand in number and northern ones subside.

WET CLIMATE

Within the contiguous United States, Acadia's region is second only to the Pacific Northwest in terms of annual precipitation. During prime hiking season, this moisture arrives in the form of fog, rain, and an occasional thunderstorm. Acadia also receives an average annual snowfall of 60 inches (152 cm). Most snowstorms occur between December and March, but snow is possible from October through April. Many winter and early spring storms include sleet or freezing rain.

VARIABLE CONDITIONS

Acadia's weather can be unpredictable. Even in the middle of the summer, cool fall-like temperatures are not uncommon. And weather can change in an instant. Check the forecast before hitting the trails. The park has a broad array of hiking experiences. Matching your hike to the current conditions and weather will increase your safety and enjoyment. While every year is different, here are some seasonal considerations to keep in mind.

Spring. Warm April weather does not mean spring has arrived everywhere. It is not unusual for patches of snow and ice to remain on northern ridges and at high elevations into May. Many spring days have a winter chill, so be prepared to don a hat, gloves, and an extra layer. While sometimes winter-like, spring can also resemble summer. Remember to shield yourself from the sun's rays and check for ticks. Swarming blackflies usually appear between mid-May and early June. They do not like wind but thrive in heat, especially in the afternoon. Finally, prepare for the presence of water. To ensure that the worst-case scenario is wet boots, use caution at all stream crossings and use extra caution descending wet granite ledges and other moist surfaces. Consider sticking with south-facing routes in damp conditions because they tend to dry more quickly.

Summer. In summer, swarming mosquitoes, crawling ticks, and circling deerflies can be annoying or worse. Be prepared with effective repellent and head for windy, open locations to minimize encounters. These cooler destinations are also attractive on hot, humid days, but be alert for the possibility of a late-day thunderstorm. Other ways to beat the heat are to hit the trail early in the day or later in the afternoon and always drink plenty of fluids. Finally, remember there are significant elevation changes. The temperature in town and at sea level differs from that at the highest summits, especially if it is windy. Mountains can also experience dramatic changes in weather conditions—a hot, sunny day can quickly become a cool, wet one. Be sure to pack an additional layer of clothing: It is better to have and not need than to need and not have.

Autumn. Autumn hiking can be enjoyable, but days grow short and temperatures drop quickly as the sun goes down. Even during the middle of the day, it is not uncommon to experience winter-like conditions, especially in late October and November. Be sure to have plenty of warm clothing, including a winter hat and gloves. While most trails in the park are well marked and easy to follow, fallen leaves can at times obscure paths, hide rocks and other uneven surfaces, and result in wet, slippery terrain. Take your time and make sure you are following the blue blazes or small cairns marking the way. Use extra caution at water crossings and wet surfaces if the temperature is hovering around the freezing mark—sometimes there is a fine line between damp rocks and icy ones.

Winter. Winter's margin for error is slimmer than that of other seasons. Weather can mean snow, sleet, and freezing temperatures on one end, as well as sun and springlike warmth on the other. Both extremes can even happen on the same day. Carry more food, water, and clothes than you think you will need to ensure you are prepared in case of injury or other unforeseen issues. Winter hikes often take much longer than the same journey during the summer, and the days are much shorter. Surfaces are also more difficult to navigate. Always bring and expect to use snowshoes and some type

A historic stone bridge frames an ice-covered Hadlock Falls (Hike 21).

VISITING ACADIA IN WINTER

During "winter" (November 1 through April 14), park services are limited. Although campgrounds and visitor centers are closed, you can find information at the Bar Harbor Chamber of Commerce. Hiking trails remain open, but road closures, unpredictable weather, and icy conditions provide significant obstacles. Be flexible and check the park website for current conditions. Between December and March, visit after a healthy snowstorm, when fresh powder covers otherwise icy hiking trails and leads to ideal cross-country skiing on carriage roads and good snowshoeing conditions.

of ice gripper, and do not assume trailhead conditions mirror those closer to the summit. Choose narrow snowshoes with metal grips to allow maximum control and maneuverability. Remember that many trailheads are inaccessible, so check the park's website to get the latest road information.

PARK RULES AND REGULATIONS

Before heading out, visit the park's website for the latest information on rules, regulations, and other advice to make sure your hiking adventure is a safe and enjoyable one. The following will get you started.

PERMITS AND FEES

When visiting Acadia between May and October you must have and display an entrance pass on your vehicle. These can be purchased online and at park contact stations, including Hulls Cove Visitor Center, Thompson Island Information Center (on Route 3 just before reaching Mount Desert Island), Sand Beach Entrance Station on Park Loop Road, Village Green Information Center in Bar Harbor, and Schoodic Woods, Seawall, and Blackwoods Campgrounds. Many types of entrance passes are available to fit your needs.

Acadia has implemented many policies designed to protect the park's natural and cultural resources and to enhance public enjoyment. Please follow these commonsense regulations to ensure future generations can continue to experience the beauty of Acadia National Park.

Backcountry Camping. There are no primitive campsites on Acadia's hiking trails and all backcountry camping is prohibited. Camping is allowed only at developed facilities within the park.

Dogs. Unlike most national parks, Acadia is dog friendly, but rules apply. Dogs are prohibited from the park's ladder trails, public beaches (between May 15 and October 15), public buildings, and ranger-led programs. Many of the park's trails visit lakes and ponds that are public water supplies. "No swimming" rules apply to both you and your pet. Dogs must be kept on a leash no longer than 6 feet (2 m) to minimize unwelcomed interaction with other hikers, wildlife, and other dogs. Be sure your pet does not disturb or chase wildlife, and be sure to collect and properly dispose of all waste. The area enjoys clean water; please play your part in keeping it that way.

Driving in the Park. Within Acadia, follow these few basic driving rules: Park on the asphalt along one-way sections of roadway where parking is allowed, be sure to allow for at least 3 feet (1 m) of clearance when passing a bicyclist or pedestrian, use existing pullouts and parking lots, and be alert for wildlife. Some of the park's trailheads are located on numbered state highways where parking along the roadway is allowed. In all cases, look for signs and follow them accordingly. Remember, obeying posted speed limits means safety for you, other drivers, and wildlife.

Vehicle Height Restrictions. Park Loop and Stanley Brook Roads travel under many historic stone bridges. While most vehicles fit safely under these overpasses, some may not.

A carriage road along Bubble Pond provides a great view of Cadillac Mountain's west face (Hike 11).

The lowest underpass is 10 feet, 4 inches (3.2 m); others are slightly higher. If a bridge is damaged, the Park Service will cite the driver and seek restitution.

Minimizing Congestion. The Park Service asks you to minimize traffic congestion by finding an alternative destination if a parking lot is full when you arrive and to consider exploring Acadia without a vehicle by using the Island Explorer or a bicycle.

Carriage Roads. Acadia's carriage roads are multiuse recreational corridors. To facilitate safe passage for all, please follow these protocols: Bicyclists yield to everyone, all users yield to horses, and hikers should walk along the right side rather than across a road's entire width. Bicyclists should travel at safe speeds (no faster than 20 mph/30 kph), announce their passage on the left with ample warning, and be prepared to safely stop on the loose gravel surface. In the winter, stay off groomed cross-country ski trails unless skiing and wear snowshoes on other portions of the trail.

E-Bikes. Carriage roads in the park allow only one class of e-bikes—Class 1 bikes, which have motors that assist only while the rider is pedaling and do not exceed 20 mph (30 kph). As when using traditional bikes, please ride safely and yield to all other users, including horses and pedestrians. Stay to the right and give a clear warning before passing on the left.

Bates Cairns. Unique to Acadia, these cairns, which mark hiking trails across the park's granite ledges, are simple structures involving just four rocks constructed in a way to lead hikers in the correct direction. The gap between the two base rocks and the top stone points the way, which is especially useful in the fog, when blue blazes are covered by snow, or when the route is less than obvious. Avoid the temptation to add rocks, rearrange rocks, or construct new cairns. Making them bigger creates an eyesore, changing them impacts their effectiveness, and seeking more rocks often leads to trampled plants. Allow the Park Service to maintain the cairns while you spend more time enjoying the surrounding beauty.

Wildlife. To respect and help protect the park's wildlife, please refrain from feeding, approaching, or provoking any wild animals, especially snowy owls, nesting loons and turtles, and baby seals on beaches. Observe speed limits and watch for wild creatures crossing roadways.

Firewood and Campfires. Charcoal and wood fires are allowed only in Acadia's campgrounds and at designated picnic areas. All firewood must be purchased locally, so don't bring your own from home. Non-native insect pests pose a serious threat to Acadia's forests. These pests can find their way to the park on firewood from other locales. There are many local businesses that sell affordable firewood.

Firearms. The role of the responsible gun owner is to know and obey federal, state, and local laws appropriate to the park. Federal law prohibits firearms in park facilities and buildings marked with signs at public entrances.

Drones. Unmanned aircraft and drones are prohibited in the park.

SAFETY AND OUTDOOR ETIQUETTE

When you lace up your hiking boots and hit the trails at Acadia, you are responsible for your own safe and enjoyable adventure and for respecting fellow travelers—those you encounter while there and those who visit long after you have returned home.

HAZARDS

Although Acadia has top-notch safety and rescue personnel, the goal for every visitor should be to leave the park without ever partaking of these services. Begin by understanding the park's most common hazards.

Steep Terrain. Many Acadia trails traverse difficult terrain. Some of the routes are so steep that iron rungs, railings, and ladders are available to ensure safe passage. Are you new to hiking? Afraid of heights? Begin gradually, work up to the more challenging options, and learn your limitations. If given the choice, climb the steepest trail and descend the more gradual—which is especially critical on ladder routes.

Wet Terrain. When heading out after a rainy or foggy day, be extra cautious. The granite ledges where shoes grip easily on a dry day can become incredibly slick with the slightest precipitation. The same can be said for bog bridging and exposed roots. When in doubt, consider adjusting your plans. Check out a low-country trail or begin later in the day to allow the terrain to dry.

Lightning. Acadia's proximity to cold ocean waters tends to minimize thunderstorm activity. However, electrical storms are possible any time of year, especially between May and September. Since many hikes traverse exposed ridges, the threat of lightning should not be underestimated. To minimize risk, be aware of the day's weather forecast, choose a hike with minimal exposure if storms are likely, and pay attention to the sky. If you hear thunder, do your best to leave open areas and locations above tree line. When caught in a thunderstorm, it is wise to spread out so if one person is struck, others can help. If you are unable to get to cover, squat down to reduce your height, minimize your contact with the earth (only your feet should touch the ground), and avoid metal objects.

Hypothermia. While most often a threat during colder months, hypothermia can strike at any time. To protect yourself or a fellow hiker, understand early warning signs, which include poor judgment, a slight sensation of chilliness, and trouble completing simple tasks. Should these early signs go unaddressed, hypothermia can lead to more serious conditions such as uncontrolled shivering, unconsciousness, and even death. The best way to prevent hypothermia is to wear clothes that keep you warm even when they are wet and to dress in layers. Finally, eat and drink properly. Even when the temperature is cold, drinking plenty of water is critical to your health. Avoid alcohol and caffeine because both can contribute to hypothermia.

Sun Exposure and Heat. Despite the cooling influence of nearby ocean waters, daytime temperatures and humidity can rise to unsafe or uncomfortable levels in the park. At the same time, many of the trails traverse exposed ridges with little to no shade. When extreme heat is forecasted, start early in the day or later in the afternoon, avoid strenuous mountain hikes, and stay closer to the shoreline to minimize exposure. It is wise on hot, sunny days to be prepared with a hat, sunglasses, sunscreen, and at least a quart (1 liter) of water.

Water. Unless faced with extreme dehydration, do not drink water from sources found on the trail before treating it. Even seemingly clean streams could be home to microscopic bacteria that can wreak havoc on your digestive system. Treating water can be as simple as chemically purifying it with iodine tablets or pumping it through one of the many commercially available water filter systems. Rather than relying on finding clean water out on the trail, start every hike with at least a quart (1 liter) from a reliable source.

Lost and Found. While Acadia trails are well-developed and frequently traveled, being lost, injured, or stranded after dark is a possibility. Never rely on technology to save you. Cell phones cannot receive signals everywhere in the park, and even when they do, the battery may die. It is better to rely on basic outdoor skills, preparedness, common sense, and a few simple rules: It is always safer to hike with companions, so if you choose to hike alone, be sure to let someone else know your plans; study the area beforehand and bring a map to have a good understanding of the topography; keep your group together; and carry and know how to use the Ten Essentials (later in this section).

PLANT AND WILDLIFE CONCERNS

Potentially dangerous and/or poisonous animals and plants are on the top of many hikers' minds, particularly those who have not spent a lot of time outdoors. While Acadia is not known as a park with many threatening and troublesome wild creatures, there are a few that demand attention—some encounters can be life-threatening.

Insects. Some people tend to fear large animals, but the ones most likely to injure you in Acadia are small. The most common antagonists are blackflies, mosquitoes, deerflies, brown-tail moths, and yellow jackets. Since their presence varies based on the time of year, time of day, and current weather conditions, you will not encounter each of these on every hike during the year's warmer months. Still, it is possible you will encounter at least one of them if you hike between April and November. Frequently, encounters with these critters are manageable with little effort. However, if their numbers are high, you suffer allergic reactions, and/or your tolerance is low, consider using insect repellents, hats, long pants, or commercially available gear to help ease the annoyance, threat, and pain inflicted by them.

Ticks. The small critter that poses the most significant threat is the deer tick, a tiny bloodsucking parasite whose numbers have been increasing within the park. They spread Lyme disease and other less common illnesses. If left untreated, these tick-borne diseases can result in long-term health issues and even death. To avoid picking up ticks, it is helpful to tuck clothes in and wear light colors. As an added precaution, apply insect repellent to your shoes, clothing, and skin. You can minimize potential tick encounters by sticking to the middle of the trail and avoiding tall vegetation. Lastly, after every hike, do a thorough scan of your body to ensure no ticks are present and use fine-tipped tweezers to quickly and thoroughly remove any you find. While it is not uncommon to have a tick-free Acadia hike, you may find one crawling on you from early spring through late fall.

Wildlife. Acadia lacks poisonous snakes. Large predators such as coyotes, bobcats, and black bears are mostly reclusive and tend to avoid human contact. The same could be said for white-tailed deer. Although rare within Acadia, male moose can be problematic during the fall rutting season, and female moose with young can be aggressive if their space is violated. Since moose typically do not go looking for trouble, as long as you are not overly enthusiastic about getting a photo, you should remain safe. Similarly, be aware of black bear sows with young and act cautiously; they typically sense your presence first and are long gone before you arrive.

Do not let wildlife fears deter you from an Acadia hiking adventure. Use common sense with all animals (view from a distance, do not feed them, and respect their space), and you will likely avoid dangerous encounters. The animal you are most apt to be threatened by on a hike will be an unleashed dog, which can just as easily occur in your neighborhood.

Poison Ivy. Found naturally in the park but not on many hiking trails, poison ivy is a valuable part of the ecosystem, providing food and cover for birds and animals. It also plays an important role in maintaining soil quality and minimizing erosion. Unfortunately, poison ivy contains substances that, once in contact with human skin, can cause significant rashes that can last for days. While very itchy and annoying, the rash typically goes away within a week or so. In rare cases, infections or other complications can occur. Look for poison ivy growing in disturbed areas, at the edges of open fields, along roadsides, and near the shore. The park does control the spread of the plant along the Ocean Path. Should you contact poison ivy, urushiol oil from the plant can linger on your skin, clothes, gear, and pets' fur, so gently cleaning your skin, clothing and gear, and pets' fur with soap and water

Fungi thrive in Acadia National Park's moist climate.

within thirty minutes helps you avoid getting a rash. Local stores may sell products that help suppress symptoms.

THE TEN ESSENTIALS

Before hitting the trails, be prepared with proper gear. While it is often tempting to head out with less, you never know what may occur: injury, change of weather, illness, or other unforeseen issues could arise. The bottom line for any hike is to bring more than you think you will need; if nothing else, you will strengthen your back and shoulder muscles. Consider packing the following Ten Essentials, particularly when exploring Acadia's mountains and more remote areas. The point of the Ten Essentials, originated by The Mountaineers, has always been to answer two basic questions: Can you prevent emergencies and respond positively should one occur (items 1–5)? And can you safely spend a night—or more—outside (items 6–10)? Use this list as a guide and tailor it to the needs of your outing.

1. **Navigation.** Having a map of the area and knowing how to read it provides options in case of emergency. There may be multiple trails in an area that provide shorter or easier alternatives. Know where you are and how to most quickly get someplace safely if necessary. If for some reason you lose your way, a compass can also be a valuable tool to direct your travels. While the trails in this book are generally well marked and easy to follow, harsh weather and snow can sometimes obscure the route.

2. **Flashlight or headlamp.** If you are forced to spend the night outdoors or are still on the trail after sunset, artificial light can be a big help in returning safely to the trailhead. Be sure to carry spare batteries.

3. **Sun protection.** Sunglasses and sunscreen are a must throughout the year. In fact, the low angle of the sun and reflection off snow and ice can make sunglasses particularly important during colder months. Sunscreen is also

beneficial from March to October. Late winter through midspring can be the most vulnerable time of the year, when the sun is strong and bare trees provide little protection. Sun-protective clothes are a good idea as well.

4. **First-aid kit.** Cuts, stings, twisted ankles, and other ailments are distinct possibilities for even the most seasoned hiker. Kit basics include bandages; skin closures; gauze pads and dressings; roller bandage or wrap; tape; antiseptic; blister prevention and treatment supplies; nitrile gloves; tweezers; needle; nonprescription painkillers; anti-inflammatory, antidiarrheal, and antihistamine tablets; topical antibiotic; and any important personal prescriptions, including an EpiPen if you are allergic to bee or hornet venom. Knowledge of first-aid procedure can also help you know how to react in emergency situations to ensure an injured party receives necessary help.

5. **Knife/multitool.** A knife or multitool with pliers is a handy device to carry. While it may be unnecessary 99 percent of the time, the one time it is needed you will be happy to have brought one along.

6. **Fire.** Carry at least one butane lighter or matches in a waterproof container along with firestarter, such as chemical heat tabs, cotton balls soaked in petroleum jelly, or commercially prepared firestarter. Having the means to start a fire, even when sticks and brush are wet, can be a huge help in an emergency such as having to spend the night in the woods.

7. **Shelter.** In addition to a rain shell, carry a single-use bivy sack, plastic tube tent, or jumbo plastic trash bag.

8. **Extra food.** Hiking is a strenuous activity that burns calories quickly. Fill your pack with high-energy food and more than you expect to eat.

9. **Extra water.** Begin each hike with at least 20 ounces (0.6 liter) of water per person, even during cold months. Few

things put more of a damper on an otherwise enjoyable hike than headaches from dehydration.

10.**Extra clothing.** Even on the hottest days of summer, at a minimum you should carry a water-resistant layer of clothing. During colder seasons, especially while venturing above tree line, additional layers, a winter hat, and gloves are a must.

GEAR CONSIDERATIONS

Acadia hikes differ from neighborhood walks: distances will take longer than you expect, help will not come as quickly, and once you hit the trail there are no opportunities to resupply. While some of these suggestions may not be critical for the shorter, less rugged excursions outlined in the book, with increases in elevation and trail difficulty, the need for greater levels of preparedness grows exponentially. In addition to the Ten Essentials, the following gear considerations can come in handy.

Hiking Boots. No matter which trail you choose, opt for quality hiking boots or shoes to maximize your stability and grip on the surface—hiking trails are no place for street shoes. It is also desirable to seal your boots with a commercially available waterproofing material that will cause water to bead up and run off your boots, leaving your feet dry.

Hiking Poles. Many hikes in this book and throughout the region take place on rocky terrain with an abundance of stream crossings. The use of hiking poles can support tired legs on the steep descents, provide stability on uneven surfaces, and assist in tricky stream crossings.

Proper Clothing. When choosing socks or other clothing, avoid cotton, which is not the best material to wear when wet because it holds onto moisture rather than wicking it away. And, when ascending the peak's higher summits, be sure to have at least one additional layer. This will keep you warm in the cooler temperatures and steadier winds you are likely to encounter.

Insect repellent. In warmer months, throw some insect repellent into your pack—it could be the difference between a pleasant and painful excursion.

Fun Additions. While not safety related, having a camera and binoculars can add a lot of enjoyment to a hiking adventure. Similarly, books that help you identify birds, wildlife, trees, mushrooms, and wildflowers can add many new dimensions to the journey.

PICK THE RIGHT HIKE

Many factors go into picking the right hike. If you or someone in your party is relatively new to hiking or unfamiliar with the park, begin on one of the easier hikes before tackling a more strenuous one. If the forecast calls for precipitation or if trails are slick, be flexible and adapt—these are perfect days to explore the park's more hidden natural gems. Not surprisingly, many visitors are drawn to a small number of very busy trails. If you are looking for a little solitude, you may want to choose popular hikes only during the spring or fall shoulder seasons. Most popular trails have comparable alternatives that offer a quieter option on the park's busiest days. If waiting until a different time of year is impossible, get an early start or head up the trail later in the afternoon.

ALWAYS HAVE A BACKUP PLAN

Upon reaching a trailhead, you may discover a full parking area. This is mostly an issue along Park Loop Road, but other locations also have limited parking. You may encounter this anytime during the summer, during peak fall foliage, or on weekends in the spring or fall. Rather than parking illegally or waiting for a spot to open, be prepared with a backup plan. Acadia has many trails to explore. Choose Plan B and then return to the original destination at a different time.

OUTDOOR ETIQUETTE

With more folks enjoying hiking each year, the need for outdoor ethics has never been greater. Few experiences on a hike are more frustrating, for example, than seeing a mountainside that is eroded due to hikers taking shortcuts or having a peaceful day in the woods interrupted by a loud group. These experiences can leave a sour taste after an otherwise glorious day outdoors. In some cases, these activities violate the rules that govern the park; but more importantly, these activities diminish the experiences of other hikers or may negatively impact natural resources for years to come.

To ensure that we all can enjoy the same opportunity to renew our spirits in the wilds of Acadia, each of us must commit to basic outdoor ethical principles. The Leave No Trace Center for Outdoor Ethics, a national nonprofit organization dedicated to promoting and inspiring responsible outdoor recreation through education, research, and partnerships, has developed seven simple principles all hikers should follow.

The Ocean Path (Hike 3) passes many of Acadia's most-visited sites.

Plan Ahead and Prepare. This includes knowing applicable regulations and special concerns for each area visited; being prepared for extreme weather, hazards, and emergencies; scheduling trips to avoid times of high use; and understanding how to use a map, guidebook, and compass.

Travel and Camp on Durable Surfaces. Durable surfaces mean using established trails, rock, gravel, or snow. Also, walking single file in the middle of the trail, even when it's wet or muddy, minimizes erosion. Remaining on the trail is especially important for the high-elevation hikes described in this book that use trails surrounded by fragile vegetation. Backcountry camping in Acadia is prohibited. Camping is limited to Blackwoods, Seawall, Wildwood Stables, Schoodic Woods, and Duck Harbor Campgrounds.

Dispose of Waste Properly. Follow the basic rule of waste disposal: pack it in and pack it out. When depositing solid human waste, dig a small hole 6 to 8 inches (15 to 20 cm) deep at least 200 feet (60 m) from water or trails. Cover and disguise the hole when finished. Pack out toilet paper.

Leave What You Find. You are not the first to visit any of these places and likely will not be the last. Preserve the experience for others who follow by examining, but not touching, cultural or historic structures and artifacts; leaving rocks, plants, and other natural objects as you find them; avoiding the introduction or transportation of non-native species; and not building structures, furniture, or cairns.

Minimize Campfire Impacts. Lightweight stoves and candle lanterns have less impact than campfires. Where fires are permitted, use established fire rings and keep fires small. Only use sticks from the ground that can be broken by hand. Burn all wood to ash, and pour water on the ashes to be sure the campfire is completely out.

Respect Wildlife. Wildlife is best observed from a distance and should never be fed. Feeding wildlife damages their health, alters natural behaviors, and exposes them to predators and other dangers. Protect wildlife and your food by storing rations and trash securely. Control pets with a leash or leave them at home.

Be Considerate of Other Visitors. Respect other visitors and protect the quality of their experience. Be courteous and yield to other users on the trail. Let nature's sounds prevail—avoid loud voices and noises.

And to these, add an additional principle we should all keep in mind:

Think Before You Post. When sharing the day's adventure on social media, be sure to view your potential communications through a leave-no-trace lens by modeling responsible outdoor recreation in your posts.

SUGGESTED ITINERARIES

These five suggested itineraries include daylong schedules for each of the park's three sections as well as three-day adventures for Mount Desert Island and Isle au Haut.

ONE DAY: MOUNT DESERT ISLAND

It is tough to see Mount Desert Island in a single day, but this circuit explores Acadia's oldest and most well-known features. The best way to complete the tour during the summer is by using the Island Explorer service.

- Hulls Cove Visitor Center: Grab a park brochure and hop on an Island Explorer bus heading to Park Loop Road.
- Sieur de Monts Spring: Tour the Wild Gardens of Acadia, learn about George Dorr, and take a short walk along the Jesup Path (see Hike 6).
- Ocean Drive: Explore the island's most famous beach, then venture along the Ocean Path to Thunder Hole, Otter Cliff, and Otter Point for breathtaking scenery (see Hike 3). The more adventurous can add a detour to Great Head (see Hike 1), the Beehive (see Hike 2), or Gorham Mountain (see Hike 3).

- Jordan Pond: Book a table at the Jordan Pond House in advance, dine on tea and popovers, then take a relaxing jaunt around the pond (see Hike 15). If time and energy permit, scale South Bubble to see the park's most famous glacial erratic and some glorious views.
- Dinner and sunset: Upon returning to Hulls Cove, head to Bar Harbor for a seafood dinner and, with a vehicle reservation in hand, drive up Cadillac Summit Road to capture the setting sun (see www.recreation.gov for reservations).

ONE DAY: ISLE AU HAUT

After enjoying a hearty breakfast in Stonington, grab the midmorning passenger ferry to Duck Harbor.

- Morning ride: Bundle up for an oft-foggy trip through Maine's famed Merchant Row and its abundant lobster buoys while scanning the surrounding waters for porpoises, harbor seals, and guillemots.
- Western Head: Explore the Western Head Trail's remote scenic bluffs, marvel at crashing surf along the rugged Cliff Trail, and stop to admire the Goat Trail's inviting cobble beaches (see Hike 33).
- Ebens Head: Enjoy an early afternoon picnic atop Ebens Head (see Hike 34), but make sure you leave enough time to catch the ferry back at the Duck Harbor landing.
- Afternoon voyage: With a little luck the return trip will be a bit warmer, allowing you to soak up the sun's rays while capturing scenic shots of Penobscot Bay.

ONE DAY: SCHOODIC PENINSULA

One day provides a good opportunity to capture Schoodic Peninsula's unique features and stunning natural beauty.

- Lower Harbor: From the Schoodic Woods Ranger Station, descend to the shores of Lower Harbor (see Hike 37), where

belted kingfishers perch atop evergreen trees before plung-
ing into the water in search of prey.

- Schoodic Point: Snap a photo or two (or more) of the
  crashing waves pounding the colorful granite shoreline
  and the towering peaks of Mount Desert Island rising
  across the bay.
- Schoodic Head: Leave the water's edge to see the surrounding bays, islands, and peninsulas from above by
  scrambling to the top of The Anvil and Schoodic Head
  (see Hike 39) before looping back to the shore.

THREE DAYS: MOUNT DESERT ISLAND

Most hikes on Mount Desert Island are half-day treks,
allowing for multiple destinations each day. There
are many combinations from which to choose while sprin-
kling in other sites frequented by more casual park visitors.
For the following three-day itinerary, you begin along the
popular Park Loop Road, spend a day on the island's quieter
side, and then finish in the heart of Acadia's vast hiking trail
network. Along the way, enjoy a diversity of trail experiences
as well as a variety of natural features.

Day One: Park Loop Road

- Ladder trail: If you can deal with precipitous ledges, scale
  the Beehive Trail (see Hike 2) for an exhilarating start to
  the day.
- Ocean Path: Enjoy an easy stroll along the Ocean Path
  (see Hike 3) from Sand Beach to Otter Point for incredible
  coastal scenery.
- Jordan Pond: Book a table at the Jordan Pond House to
  enjoy tea and popovers along with exquisite views; then
  take a walk along the scenic shoreline (see Hike 15).
- Cadillac Mountain: Make a reservation for a drive to the
  top of Acadia and the breathtaking panoramic views that
  await (see www.recreation.gov for reservations).

Low tide near Ship Harbor (Hike 31)

Day Two: Southwest Harbor

- Long Pond: From the shores of Long Pond, head east for a loop over Beech Mountain's granite ridges (see Hike 27) or west up the rugged slopes of Mansell Mountain (see Hike 28).
- Bass Harbor: Head to the shore to frame the Bass Harbor Head Lighthouse and picturesque Blue Hill Bay in the background to capture an iconic image of Maine.
- Nature trails: Pack your binoculars and walk softly while discovering the diverse coastal habitats around Ship Harbor (see Hike 31) and the Wonderland Trail (see Hike 32).

Day Three: Northeast Harbor

- Sargent Mountain: You cannot go wrong with any of the available options, so pick your route to the top of the park's highest roadless summit and the alluring granite ridges that surround it (see Hikes 18, 21, 22, or 23).
- Flower artistry: Tour the Land & Garden Preserve's historic Asticou Azalea and Thuya Gardens, two of the region's more beautiful reminders of the mark left by the Rockefellers and other philanthropic families with proud traditions on Mount Desert Island.

THREE DAYS: ISLE AU HAUT

Prepare in advance to ensure you secure a two-night Duck Harbor camping reservation—most nights are booked soon after they become available in early April (note there is a three-night limit). If you are one of the lucky ones, here is a great way to maximize your three days on this remote and rugged island.

Day One

- Duck Harbor: Take the midmorning passenger ferry from Stonington to Duck Harbor. Arrive around 11:00 AM, sign in, and set up your lean-to for the two nights.
- Duck Harbor Mountain: There is no better way to get a sense of your location than by scampering up and over the very steep slopes of Duck Harbor Mountain (see Hike 35).
- Campground: Enjoy a quiet dinner and, weather permitting, a wonderful sunset over Penobscot Bay.

Day Two

- Western Head: Follow the trail south around the rocks and cliff-bound shores of Western Head and then north to the inviting waters of Merchant Cove (see Hike 33).

Exploring the Land & Garden Preserve is a good addition to any Mount Desert Island itinerary.

- Bowditch: Continue your trek into the island's forested center, across the top of Bowditch Mountain, and then loop back to Duck Harbor along the edge of Moores Harbor (see Hike 36).
- Stargazing: With little artificial light to contend with, marvel at the Milky Way's celestial display while resting your tired legs after a long day on the trails.

Day Three
- Ebens Head: Start early on your final day and listen for bird activity along the way to a scenic bluff on Duck Harbor's north shore (see Hike 34).
- Ferry back: Pack up your gear, grab the late-morning passenger ferry, and relax on a pleasant voyage through Maine's famed Merchant Row en route to Stonington.

HOW TO USE THIS GUIDE

Acadia has a remarkable network of hiking trails—sometimes offering many options to the same destination. This can be overwhelming, especially to those new to the park. To help organize your hiking adventures, this book focuses on trailheads and Island Explorer stops.

From the various starting points, individual hike descriptions showcase a recommended journey. The destination may be the same or the route may partially coincide with another hike described in the book. This approach allows you to alter plans should you find a full parking lot. Similarly, you can decide which route is most preferable to a desired summit: the gradual one or the more challenging one.

Most of the hikes in the book provide additional information on how you might choose to alter the described route. In some cases, the descriptions explain how you can combine two or more hikes. When using the Island Explorer service, combining multiple hikes into one becomes more doable—get dropped off at one trailhead and picked up at another.

The book uses numerous classifications in each individual hike to assist you. The first is the **geographic region**. All forty hikes in the book fall into one of eight regions: Frenchman Bay and Ocean Drive, Dorr and Cadillac Mountains, Jordan Pond, Northeast Harbor, Southwest Harbor, Western Mountain and Bass Harbor, Isle au Haut, and Schoodic Peninsula.

OPPOSITE: *Sargent Mountain Pond sits high atop the ridge (Hike 18).*

While these are well-known geographic terms, they do not fit into a regional classification used by the park.

Next, look closely at the hike's **distance**, **elevation gain**, and **high point**. These values are listed in both imperial and metric units. In combination, the length of a hike and its elevation gain will give an initial indication of the hike's degree of difficulty. The elevation gain is an approximate calculation adding up the distinctive climbs along the described route. Most Acadia hikes have multiple ups and downs.

Through an assessment of the distance, elevation gain, high point, and trail surface, I've assigned each hike a **difficulty rating**. Hikes are rated easy, moderate, challenging, technical, or a combination of two ratings. Technical hikes are those that have extensive ladders and iron rungs. Hikes to the park's highest peaks generally fall into the challenging category, as do treks to lower peaks with steep, exposed trails. Most excursions to lesser summits are categorized as moderate. Hikes rated easy have little to no elevation change.

The book also describes the **trail surface**. The term "uneven terrain" describes trails with exposed roots, small rocks, and other minor obstacles. Many Acadia hikes have this trait as well as granite ledges. Gentler surfaces include crushed stone, rock steps, or bog bridging. The most challenging trails have ladders.

Every hike in the book is featured on a **map**, and each description also lists the map featured in the park brochure or, for Hikes 33–39, a map specific to that region, available on the Acadia National Park website. The only exception is Schoodic Mountain (Hike 40); a map for that hike is available from the Maine Bureau of Parks and Lands. The park maps show details as well as the location of the described hike in relation to other trails and natural features.

To help you find the hike, the book provides the **GPS** coordinates (using WGS84 datum) of the trailhead.

MAP LEGEND

— 1 —	US highway
— 3 —	State highway
	Primary road
	Surface road
==========	Unpaved road
··········	Carriage road/ bike path
- - - - - -	Hiking route
············	Alternate route
- - - - - -	Other trail
←	Direction of travel
T	Trailhead
P	Parking
E	Island Explorer shuttle stop

R	Restroom
▲	Summit
▪	Building
•	Feature
🎪	Picnic area
⌒	Bridge
⬤	Campground
⬤	Vista
⬇	Wetlands
⫫	Waterfall
	River/brook/stream
- - - - -	Seasonal stream
⬭	Waterbody
▬	Park

Look under the **notes** section for unique information about the hike. This could include whether there is a restroom or a privy at the trailhead, a specific regulation for the parking area, or some other piece of information that is helpful to know before you reach the trailhead.

The route description begins with a short paragraph that focuses on the highlights you will encounter along the hike, such as a scenic mountain summit, an inviting trail section, or an alluring coastal promontory. This is designed to provide you a flavor of the hike and what makes it special.

Under **Getting There**, each hike provides **driving** directions to the parking area and, when applicable, **transit** directions to the trailhead using the Island Explorer service. In some cases, a trailhead's parking lot and bus stop are in different locations, which will be described.

Hikers scramble up the Precipice Trail (Hike 4) with the aid of iron rungs.

Look to the **On the Trail** portion to discover the recommended route for the hike. The description is designed to provide you with the necessary information to follow the prescribed course, including appropriate turns at each intersection. You will also get a feel for the hike and its different segments: the degree of difficulty, the flora and fauna you might encounter, unique natural features, historical information, and some of the scenery you are likely to see on a clear day. The level of detail does not capture every aspect of the hike, allowing you to discover some of the finer details on your own.

Many of the hikes include a section titled **Going Farther** or **Other Options**. Acadia provides a great variety of trail experiences, and most trailheads provide multiple options. These brief sections offer ways to amend the described route to help you take full advantage of everything the park has to offer.

A NOTE ABOUT SAFETY

Safety is an important concern in all outdoor activities. No guidebook can alert you to every hazard or anticipate the limitations of every reader. Therefore, the descriptions of roads, trails, routes, and natural features in this book are not representations that a particular place or excursion will be safe for your party. When you follow any of the routes described in this book, you assume responsibility for your own safety. Under normal conditions, such excursions require the usual attention to traffic, road and trail conditions, weather, terrain, the capabilities of your party, and other factors. Keeping informed on current conditions and exercising common sense are the keys to a safe, enjoyable outing.

—*Mountaineers Books*

FRENCHMAN BAY AND OCEAN DRIVE

Frenchman Bay's cold waters and collection of islands form the eastern edge of Mount Desert Island. Near the mouth of the bay, Champlain Mountain steeply rises more than 1000 feet (300 m), forming an impressive granite ridge that descends south to Ocean Drive and the rocky shores of Otter Point and Great Head.

This popular corner of Acadia offers hiking opportunities for all ages and abilities, from flat, crushed stone surfaces to steep scrambles up iron rungs and ladders. All paths eventually lead to high coastal bluffs or barren rocky summits where breathtaking ocean views and cool breezes await. Regardless of the trail you choose, expect company, as many visitors are drawn here to visit signature park features, including Sand Beach, Thunder Hole, the Precipice, and Otter Cliff.

In season, take advantage of the Island Explorer shuttle to access this section's well-used trails. It is the best way to avoid traffic congestion and filled parking lots. The buses are also a convenient way to visit other popular destinations along Park Loop Road.

OPPOSITE: *View of Great Head from Otter Cliff (Hike 3)*

1   GREAT HEAD AND SAND BEACH

Distance: 2-mile (3.2-km) loop
Elevation gain: 280 feet (85 m)
High point: 145 feet (44 m)
Difficulty: Easy to moderate
Trail surface: Bog bridging, rock steps, granite ledges, and uneven terrain
Map: Park brochure
GPS: 44.329898°N, 68.183691°W
Notes: No dogs on beach mid-June through early September; restroom at trailhead

> This popular swimming spot and small but prominent peninsula combine to form a pleasant loop featuring stunning coastal views, cool breezes, and opportunities to spot common eiders feeding in the surf and bald eagles soaring high above.

GETTING THERE

Driving: From the Hulls Cove Visitor Center, follow signs pointing to Park Loop Road and drive south 3 miles (4.8 km) to a three-way intersection. Continue left on Park Loop Road (one-way traffic only) and drive south 5.4 miles (8.7 km) to the Sand Beach Entrance Station. Drive another 0.5 mile (0.8 km) to the Sand Beach parking area on the left. To drive to this trailhead during peak times, you may need a reservation through www.recreation.gov. However, the reservation provides road access only and not a guaranteed parking spot. To ensure your hike begins at the trailhead, use the transit option.

Transit: From late June to mid-October, Island Explorer buses stop at this trailhead throughout the day.

ON THE TRAIL

At the parking lot's southern end, descend stairs leading to the beach and head east across the sandy expanse. Looking left over Beehive Lagoon enjoy views of its namesake mountain's imposing ledge-covered slopes, often reflected in the water below. To the right scan for sea ducks, grebes, and loons feeding in the rolling waves. Stay close to the shore for the most solid footing; the waves are usually tame.

In 0.2 mile (0.3 km), reach the end of the beach. Depending on the tide and time of year, you may need to cross a small stream before reaching the signpost marking the Great Head Trail. Ascend rock steps to a junction and the start of the 1.6-mile (2.6-km) loop.

Stay right and scramble up the granite ledges that rise quickly to splendid aerial views of the beach. Watch your footing while making your way to a ridgetop trail junction. Continue right on the main route, which parallels the shoreline while descending 0.2 mile (0.3 km) to the peninsula's

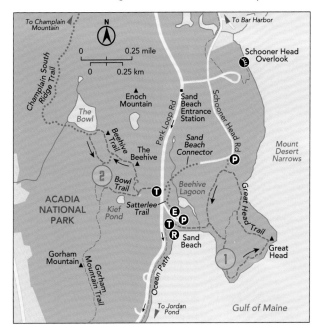

The Great Head Trail features views of the Beehive and Sand Beach.

southern tip. Marvel at ocean vistas along the way, including rugged scenes southwest to Otter Cliff.

Swinging left, the route begins a 0.3-mile (0.5-km) trek to Great Head's 145-foot (44-m) high point. Carefully follow the meandering blue-blazed trail around small coves, over rocky knolls, and past unmarked paths leading to the shore.

A final climb rises atop the stunning promontory, well above the pounding waves. This idyllic spot is often an oasis in hot summer temperatures and, unless shrouded in a thick fog, offers sweeping views across Mount Desert Narrows to Schoodic Peninsula's distant shores. Notice the remains of a stone tower a local family constructed here in the early 1900s. In a bygone era, the family invited guests to visit their tearoom and observatory.

The journey resumes northwest along the Great Head Trail. While rocky at first, this portion of the circuit soon enjoys more level terrain. In 0.3 mile (0.5 km) reach an intersection where a path exits left, cutting across the peninsula. Skip this shorter but more challenging route back to Sand Beach. Instead, stay straight on the Great Head Trail for a more relaxing conclusion.

Hike north 0.3 mile (0.5 km) to another intersection, where a path diverts right to an alternative access point. Stay left as the mostly flat path meanders south toward Sand Beach. Upon completing the circuit, notice the large millstone on the right—another historical artifact from the family who owned this property a century ago.

Stay right, descend the staircase to the beach, and then return across the open expanse to conclude the hike. If it's hot, consider taking a dip. Those hardy enough to enter the cold waters will find Sand Beach waters refreshing.

OTHER OPTIONS

If you are visiting the park with your dog between mid-June and September, access Great Head from the trailhead at the southern end of Schooner Head Road. You can drive to the parking area or get there by hiking 0.4 mile (0.6 km) from the Sand Beach parking area. Begin the hike on the Satterlee Trail, swing right onto the Sand Beach Connector, and then follow Schooner Head Road to the Great Head Trail.

2   THE BEEHIVE

Distance: 1.4-mile (2.3-km) loop
Elevation gain: 600 feet (185 m)
High point: 538 feet (164 m)
Difficulty: Technical (nontechnical option)
Trail surface: Granite ledges, ladders, and uneven terrain
Map: Park brochure
GPS: 44.329898°N, 68.183691°W
Notes: Dogs prohibited on the Beehive Trail; restroom near trailhead

> Featuring a challenging, near-vertical route requiring hikers to ascend iron rungs and ladders affixed to solid granite, this popular climb to mesmerizing ocean panoramas is a short but sweet choice for those willing to brave the sharp drop-offs.

GETTING THERE

Driving: From the Hulls Cove Visitor Center, follow signs pointing to Park Loop Road and drive south 3 miles (4.8 km) to a three-way intersection. Continue left on Park Loop Road (one-way traffic only) and drive south 5.4 miles (8.7 km) to the Sand Beach Entrance Station. Drive another 0.5 mile (0.8 km) to the Sand Beach parking area on the left. To drive to this trailhead during peak times, you may need a reservation through www .recreation.gov. However, the reservation provides road access only and not a guaranteed parking spot. To ensure your hike begins at the trailhead, use the transit option.

Transit: From late June to mid-October, Island Explorer buses stop at this trailhead throughout the day.

ON THE TRAIL

To reach the trailhead, follow the parking lot entranceway back to Park Loop Road. Turn right and follow the pavement to quickly reach the Bowl Trail on the left. This very rocky

A hiker carefully navigates the Beehive Trail.

path begins at a moderate grade. In 0.2 mile (0.3 km) arrive at a junction with the Beehive Trail to start the loop.

Turn right and slowly wind up the increasingly sheer mountain face. Geologically, the Beehive is a classic roche moutonnée, with a gradual northern slope and a steeper southern one. Slow-moving glaciers shaped it thousands of years ago as water melted, filled in cracks, froze, and dislodged rocks. To navigate the difficult terrain, the Beehive Trail follows a well-designed route across metal bridges, up ladders and iron rungs, and on the edge of the mountain's granite walls.

In spots, the slope drops off precipitously. Watch your step, take your time, and catch your breath at the limitless beauty along the way. Looking east to west, enjoy breathtaking views of Schoodic Point, Mount Desert Narrows, Great Head, Sand Beach, and Otter Cliff. The 0.3-mile (0.5-km) scramble eventually crests the Beehive's 538-foot (164-m) summit, where a more expansive, albeit less dramatic, panorama awaits.

Proceed northwest along the ridge (for safety reasons the park asks that you not descend the way you came up). No longer technical, the route weaves through the stunted pine forest across mostly open granite ledges. In 0.1 mile (0.2 km), a shortcut departs left, connecting with the Bowl Trail. Continue straight and easily ascend to the top of an unnamed peak to enjoy impressive views of Champlain Mountain to the north.

Carefully descend the rocky path to the Bowl, a secluded pond nestled high on the ridge. Scan the waters for wood duck or other waterfowl feeding along the shore and listen for the haunting calls of hermit thrush echoing from the surrounding evergreen forest. The path swings left and hugs the pond's shore en route to a three-way intersection.

Turn left onto the Bowl Trail to complete the second half of the 1.4-mile (2.3-km) hike. After a brief climb, it descends through an attractive birch forest. While the decline is steady, the footing is sound. Stay on the Bowl Trail as one path departs left to the Beehive and two others leave right toward Gorham Mountain. Shortly after skirting the edge of Kief Pond, a small forested wetland on the right, reach the base of the Beehive Trail. Continue straight and retrace your steps to the start.

GOING FARTHER

From the Bowl, consider adding the 2.6-mile (4.2-km) roundtrip trek to Champlain Mountain. The 650-foot (198-m) climb is challenging at first but moderates near the summit. This scenic route along the Champlain South Ridge Trail showcases additional expansive views.

OTHER OPTIONS

If the steep route is too daunting or you are hiking with a dog, amend the described hike by using the short connector that departs the Bowl Trail into the saddle between the two Beehive summits.

3   GORHAM MOUNTAIN AND OCEAN PATH

Distance: **2.8-mile (4.5-km) loop**
Elevation gain: **550 feet (170 m)**
High point: **525 feet (161 m)**
Difficulty: **Moderate**
Trail surface: **Crushed stone, granite ledges, and uneven terrain**
Map: **Park brochure**
GPS: **44.316602°N, 68.191689°W**
Notes: **Restrooms along route (Sand Beach and Thunder Hole)**

> A good tune-up before tackling more challenging park terrain, this moderately difficult loop hike showcases breathtaking ocean vistas from high, exposed granite ledges. You'll also get more intimate views of crashing surf at some of Acadia's most photogenic and visited locations.

GETTING THERE

Driving: From the Hulls Cove Visitor Center, follow signs pointing to Park Loop Road and drive south 3 miles (4.8 km) to a three-way intersection. Continue left on Park Loop Road (one-way traffic only) and drive south 5.4 miles (8.7 km) to the Sand Beach Entrance Station. Drive another 1.5 miles (2.4 km) to the parking area on the right. To drive to this trailhead during peak times, you may need a reservation through www .recreation.gov. However, the reservation provides road access only and not a guaranteed parking spot. To ensure your hike begins at the trailhead, use the transit option.

Transit: From late June to mid-October, Island Explorer buses pass this trailhead throughout the day. Since this

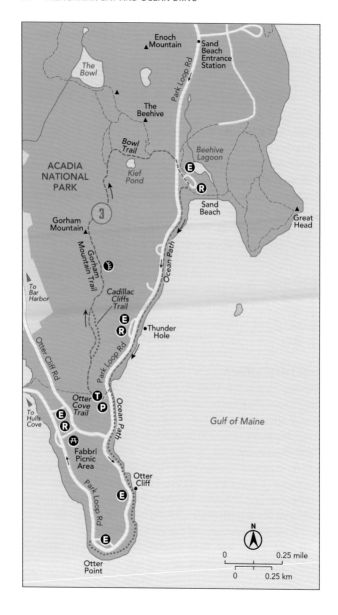

trailhead is not a regular stop, inform the driver where you want to get off the bus.

ON THE TRAIL

The Gorham Mountain Trail begins gradually on rocks that are often slippery. In 0.1 mile (0.2 km), at an intersection where the Otter Cove Trail leads left to Blackwoods Campground, bear right and hike 0.2 mile (0.3 km) to a second junction. Here, two options avail themselves. To the right, the Cadillac Cliffs Trail lures hikers 0.3 mile (0.5 km) through caves, under impressive ledges, and up rock stairs. The Gorham Mountain Trail proceeds 0.2 mile (0.3 km) straight, across less dramatic, more straightforward terrain. You cannot go wrong whichever you choose.

After the two paths reconnect, a more aggressive climb ensues. Before long, reach the first of many viewpoints. Enjoy the sights and sounds of the nearby ocean: the magnificent rockbound coast below and raucous calls of herring and black-backed gulls gliding on steady breezes above.

The final stretch to Gorham Mountain's 525-foot (161-m) summit is less arduous. Once atop the wide-open high point, 0.8 mile (1.3 km) from the start, enjoy views of Cadillac, Dorr, and Champlain Mountains towering to the north.

Remain on the Gorham Mountain Trail as it continues north. The route gradually descends while weaving around and across granite ledges. Straight ahead enjoy scenes of the Beehive's steep southern slopes. Upon entering a white birch forest, stay straight at an intersection and then quickly reach a junction with the Bowl Trail.

Turn right and descend 0.3 mile (0.5 km) to Park Loop Road. Briefly follow the pavement right and then turn left into the entranceway to the Sand Beach parking area. Behind the restrooms and Island Explorer bus stop, find the start of the Ocean Path. Before heading up this well-trodden trail,

Spring fog lingers around Sand Beach and Great Head.

consider checking out Sand Beach—a worthwhile diversion (see Hike 1).

The Ocean Path leads 2.2 miles (3.5 km) from Sand Beach to Otter Point. It passes some of Acadia's most-visited natural features. To return to the Gorham Mountain Trailhead, hike the path's northernmost mile.

From Sand Beach, the wide route climbs steps before leveling off near and then paralleling the road. The next 0.9 mile (1.4 km) is much easier. Occasionally, spurs diverge left off the main trail, affording closer views of the rocky coast. These side options include the very popular Thunder Hole, where the incoming surf crashes within a narrow chasm along the shoreline. When leaving the Ocean Path, use caution and watch your footing, especially if the rocks are wet.

At the sign for the Gorham Mountain Trail, turn right. Carefully cross the road to complete the loop back to the parking area. If using the Island Explorer, you will need to flag down a bus here or go farther to a scheduled bus stop (see Going Farther).

GOING FARTHER

Explore the Ocean's Path southern half. From the Gorham Mountain Trailhead, the 1.2-mile (1.9-km) route proceeds south to the top of Otter Cliff's scenic ledges, descends quickly back to the shore, and ends at Otter Point. You will find endless photo opportunities along the way, as well as bus stops at Otter Cliff and Otter Point.

4   CHAMPLAIN MOUNTAIN AND PRECIPICE

Distance: 2.7-mile (4.3-km) loop
Elevation gain: 1100 feet (335 m)
High point: 1063 feet (324 m)
Difficulty: Technical
Trail surface: Granite ledges, ladders, crushed stone, and uneven terrain
Map: Park brochure
GPS: 44.349453°N, 68.187939°W
Notes: Dogs are prohibited; trail typically closes seasonally to protect nesting falcons

> Not to be underestimated, the Precipice Trail scales a seemingly insurmountable rocky slope with the aid of ladders, iron rungs, and railings. Hikers able to overcome the dizzying heights are rewarded with extraordinary bird's-eye views of the park.

GETTING THERE

Driving: From the Hulls Cove Visitor Center, follow signs pointing to Park Loop Road and drive south 3 miles (4.8 km) to a three-way intersection. Continue left on Park Loop Road (one-way traffic only) and drive south 4.6 miles (7.4 km) to the parking area on the right. Because overflow parking is limited, the transit option, when available, is the better choice.

Scaling iron rungs and ladders leads to scenes of Frenchman Bay.

Transit: From late June to mid-October, Island Explorer buses pass the trailhead throughout the day, but remember that most years the trail is closed until early August to protect nesting falcons. Since this trailhead is not a regular stop, inform the driver where you want to get off the bus.

ON THE TRAIL

Begin at the large kiosk, where signs sufficiently warn of the Precipice Trail's difficulty. There is no warm-up as the trail aggressively climbs the granite slope. In 0.1 mile (0.2 km), reach the first difficult challenge, sometimes referred to as the "eliminator." This small ledge with iron rungs requires extra care. If you find this obstacle difficult, consider turning around and choosing a different hike. Over the next 0.3 mile (0.5 km) the hike lacks similar acrobatic maneuvers but is far from easy.

After ascending a boulder field, weave through small rock tunnels and then rise to the side of a granite wall. The route parallels the sheer face along a narrow shelf, but railings provide extra protection. Continue climbing, with an occasional descent, to an open ledge at a junction with the Orange and Black Path.

This is a good place to bail if you are having second thoughts; otherwise bear left on the Precipice Trail. While the final 0.4 mile (0.6 km) to the summit is the most challenging, it begins with good footing. Then, in 0.1 mile (0.2 km), the real fun begins. Carefully ascend the ladders, rock steps, and iron rungs. As you wind up the smooth granite wall, hold the available railings, take your time, watch your step, and marvel at the stunning views of Mount Desert Narrows, Schoodic Point, and Great Head.

After briefly leveling, a final steep pitch leads to Champlain Mountain's 1063-foot (324-m) summit and a 360-degree panorama, which includes Cadillac and Dorr Mountains to the west. Scan the skies for the endangered peregrine falcons that nest on the mountain's steep slopes. These sleek raptors can reach incredible speeds when descending upon vulnerable prey.

Begin your descent on the Champlain North Ridge Trail (for safety reasons the park asks that you not descend the way you came up). Although not easy, it is far less technical

HIKING ISLAND EXPLORER STYLE

Using the free Island Explorer bus service is a great way to avoid filled parking lots and busy roads. As a bonus, a seemingly endless array of hike options are available to you that begin at one trailhead and end at another. You can often start off as ambitiously as you like and avail yourself of multiple opportunities to shorten plans when necessary. Look for suggested Island Explorer routes throughout the book and feel inspired to design your own adventure.

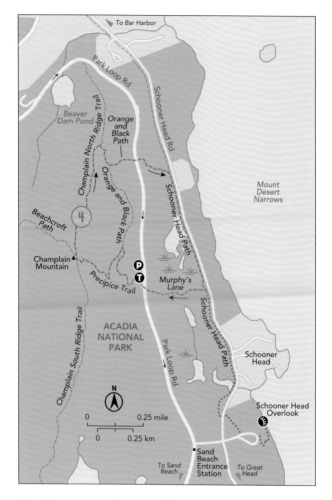

than the route up. For 0.6 mile (1 km), the blue-blazed trail weaves down the steep granite ledges in and out of the pine forest. Watch your footing and enjoy the scenes across Bar Harbor to Schoodic Mountain rising above the northern shores of Frenchman Bay.

At a cedar post, turn right onto the Orange and Black Path, which rises to a scenic vista before dropping 0.1 mile (0.2 km) to a three-way junction. To the right, one branch of the Orange and Black Path connects with the Precipice Trail. Turn left and follow the other branch as it descends steeply 0.2 mile (0.3 km) to Park Loop Road.

Carefully cross the pavement to rejoin the Orange and Black Path. The footing becomes much easier as the route gradually drops. In 0.2 mile (0.3 km), bear right onto the mostly level Schooner Head Path. The journey's final stretch is by far the easiest. Head south between the paved road and an expansive wetland and in 0.5 mile (0.8 km) turn right onto Murphy's Lane. Through a pleasant hardwood forest, this path winds 0.3 mile (0.5 km) back to the Precipice Trailhead.

GOING FARTHER

From the Murphy's Lane junction, follow the Schooner Head Path south 0.7 mile (1.1 km) to a parking area and then descend gently 0.1 mile (0.2 km) to an overlook of the rocky head on the edge of Mount Desert Narrows.

5 CHAMPLAIN MOUNTAIN AND BEACHCROFT

Distance: 2.4 miles (3.9 km)
Elevation gain: 1050 feet (320 m)
High point: 1063 feet (324 m)
Difficulty: Moderate to challenging
Trail surface: Rock steps, granite ledges, crushed stone, and uneven terrain
Map: Park brochure
GPS: 44.359079°N, 68.205916°W
Notes: Dogs not recommended on the Beachcroft Path's upper section

Offering great rewards for the effort, this well-manicured route rises methodically to scenic bluffs. A final scramble up granite leads to the mostly barren summit named in honor of the first French explorer to marvel at this L'île des Monts Déserts.

GETTING THERE

From the Bar Harbor Village Green at the intersection of Mount Desert Street and Main Street, follow Route 3 (Main Street) south. Drive 2.2 miles (3.5 km) and then turn right into the parking area.

ON THE TRAIL

Follow the unmarked path that parallels Route 3 about 100 feet (30 m) south to the Beachcroft Path. Turn left and carefully cross Route 3. Use caution, as the traffic moves quickly here. Once across the pavement, find a cedar post where the trail enters the forest.

The Beachcroft Path quickly transforms into a work of art, where flat stones and rock steps lead through the hardwood forest. While the mountain slope is steep, the route winds up a series of switchbacks that reduce the incline. Catch your breath at the many outlooks, each offering more expansive views than the last. Reach the most impressive vista 0.7 mile (1.1 km) from the start. Atop a wide bluff, the aerial shots of The Tarn far below and the ledge-covered slopes of Dorr Mountain across the valley are stunning.

The path rises into the forest and wraps around the southern slopes of Huguenot Head, a trailless knob. A brief descent leads to a forested wetland and a good opportunity to spot resident songbirds. Look for yellow-rumped warblers flitting around among the dense vegetation. Aptly named, this diminutive songbird often perches and sings near treetops.

OPPOSITE: *A hiker takes advantage of the Beachcroft Path's stonework.*

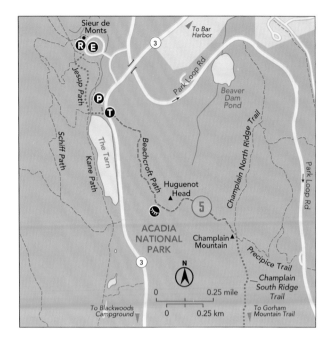

The final 0.4 mile (0.6 km) is the hike's most challenging section. Rise steeply through the thinning pine forest to reach the 1063-foot (324-m) summit. The mountain is named for Samuel de Champlain, the French explorer who was the first European to describe the lands that have become Acadia National Park. On his 1604 voyage from the Saint Croix River to Cape Cod, Champlain noted the island's treeless summits. His namesake peak affords breathtaking views of Frenchman Bay, Schoodic Peninsula, Cadillac Mountain, the Cranberry Isles, and surrounding natural features in all directions.

Enjoy the sights and sounds before retracing your steps to the start. Take your time and watch your step, especially just below the summit. If the surface is wet or icy, the upper ledges can be difficult to navigate.

GOING FARTHER

Take advantage of the Island Explorer to traverse Champlain Mountain's southern ridge. Begin at Sieur de Monts (see "Sieur de Monts" sidebar in the Dorr and Cadillac Mountains chapter), where the Jesup Path leads south 0.3 mile (0.5 km) to The Tarn and the start of the Beachcroft Path. Follow the described route to the summit and then follow the Champlain South Ridge and Bowl Trails 1.6 miles (2.6 km) to the Gorham Mountain Trail (see Hike 3).

Either remain on the Bowl Trail or follow the Gorham Mountain Trail. Both lead to Park Loop Road where you can grab an Island Explorer at the Sand Beach, Thunder Hole, Otter Cliff, or Otter Point stops. Consider a walk along the Ocean Path before catching a bus back to your car.

DORR AND CADILLAC MOUNTAINS

The highest summit on America's Eastern Seaboard, Cadillac Mountain is one of the first places in the country to welcome the sun's rays. Its gradual north and south ridges feature miles of exposed granite, bordered with steep slopes to the east and west. Cadillac Mountain and nearby Dorr Mountain dominate the eastern half of Mount Desert Island and can be seen from miles away.

With few exceptions, the trails that traverse Cadillac and Dorr Mountains are challenging—some very popular and others more lightly traveled. The paths traverse scenic ridgelines, hidden valleys, and rugged slopes. From most trailheads, the best option is to combine multiple trails into a loop that visits each of these natural features.

This popular section of the park lures many visitors to two locales: Sieur de Monts Spring and the Cadillac Mountain summit. Take advantage of the Island Explorer to access the trails departing Sieur de Monts and be prepared for many fellow travelers atop Cadillac—most arriving by car. Both spots have numerous interpretive signs highlighting interesting features.

OPPOSITE: *The Canon Brook Trail showcases views of Champlain Mountain (Hike 9).*

6 KEBO MOUNTAIN

Distance: 2.9-mile (4.7-km) loop
Elevation gain: 450 feet (140 m)
High point: 407 feet (124 m)
Difficulty: Moderate
Trail surface: Bog bridging, crushed stone, granite ledges, and uneven terrain
Map: Park brochure
GPS: 44.362694°N, 68.207685°W
Notes: Restroom at trailhead

> A good early-morning or late-afternoon excursion, this mostly forested half-day hike visits many wildlife habitats, offering opportunities to spot a wide range of wildflowers, birds, and geologic formations.

GETTING THERE

Driving: From the Bar Harbor Village Green at the intersection of Mount Desert Street and Main Street, follow Route 3 (Main Street) south. Drive 2.1 miles (3.4 km) and turn right. In 0.1 mile (0.2 km), bear left into the Sieur de Monts parking area. Because parking is limited, the transit option, when available, is the best choice.

   Transit: From late June to mid-October, Island Explorer buses stop at this trailhead throughout the day.

ON THE TRAIL

Just beyond the entrance to the Wild Gardens of Acadia, follow the Jesup Path right 0.1 mile (0.2 km) to a junction with Hemlock Road. Continue straight on the Jesup Path for 0.4 mile (0.6 km) atop a boardwalk that remains well above the forested wetland. Pause at the available benches and scan the vast grove of deciduous trees for the flora and fauna

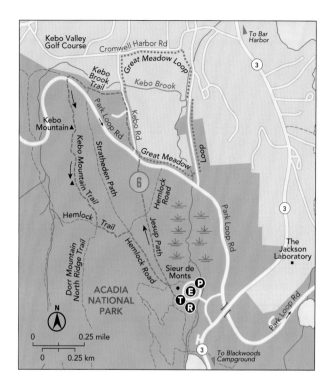

depicted on the trail's many signs describing surrounding natural features.

The boardwalk ends at a four-way intersection. Continue straight on the Jesup Path and head across the more open landscape. Offering solid footing and impressive views of Dorr Mountain's eastern slopes, the trail ends in 0.3 mile (0.5 km).

Carefully cross Park Loop Road to reach the Great Meadow Loop. On the southern edge of Bar Harbor, this circuit meanders 1.8 miles (2.9 km) across mostly easy terrain while offering distant views of the park's mountains. Turn left to hike 0.3 mile (0.5 km) of the trail. After crossing

The Jesup Path's boardwalk leads across forested wetland.

Kebo Road, the route proceeds through the hardwood forest before returning to the pavement. Parallel the road past a small cemetery. Just before reaching a golf course, turn left onto the Kebo Brook Trail.

Rising gently, this well-groomed path parallels its namesake feature and approaches Park Loop Road in 0.2 mile (0.3 km). Continue straight at a junction with the Stratheden Path and hike 0.1 mile (0.2 km) farther to reach the Kebo Mountain Trail.

Turn left, safely cross the road, and then make your way up the hike's steepest pitch to a small ledge with limited views of Bar Harbor. The remaining 0.3-mile (0.5-km) climb to Kebo Mountain's wooded 407-foot (124-m) summit is steady, but straightforward. While there were likely more views in decades past, today's scenery is mostly of the mountain's granite formations. However, catch an occasional glimpse of Cadillac Mountain through tiny gaps in the pine-dominated canopy.

From the summit, the trail winds 0.6 mile (1 km) south along the rolling ridge. On the second prominent bump, a short unmarked path leads left to a ledge with views of Frenchman Bay. Once over the trail's final knob, descend the rocky path to a four-way junction.

Turn left onto the aptly named Hemlock Trail. Watch your footing as ledge and wet stone give way to more forgiving earthen steps. In 0.2 mile (0.3 km), reach a major intersection. Turn right onto Hemlock Road to complete the hike. The final 0.4 mile (0.6 km) winds easily back to Sieur de Monts.

GOING FARTHER

When you reach the Great Meadow Loop, consider turning right to incorporate a longer section of this trail. Hike 1.5 miles (2.4 km) in a counterclockwise direction before reaching the Kebo Brook Trail on the right (just after the golf course). Resume the described hike to complete a 4.1-mile (6.6-km) loop.

7 DORR MOUNTAIN NORTH RIDGE

Distance: 3-mile (4.8-km) loop
Elevation gain: 1250 feet (380 m)
High point: 1270 feet (387 m)
Difficulty: Challenging
Trail surface: Granite ledges, rock steps, and uneven terrain
Map: Park brochure
GPS: 44.362694°N, 68.207685°W
Notes: Restroom at trailhead

> Up rock steps, past sweeping vistas, and across barren granite ledges, this hike to the mountain summit that honors the "father of Acadia National Park" is a fitting tribute to George Dorr's enduring legacy.

GETTING THERE

Driving: From the Bar Harbor Village Green at the intersection of Mount Desert Street and Main Street, follow Route 3 (Main Street) south. Drive 2.1 miles (3.4 km) and turn right. In 0.1 mile (0.2 km), bear left into the Sieur de Monts parking area. Because parking is limited, the transit option, when available, is the best choice.

Transit: From June to mid-October, Island Explorer buses stop at this trailhead throughout the day.

ON THE TRAIL

Walk beyond the nature center and follow signs pointing to the Emery Path. Once past glass-covered Sieur de Monts Spring, immediately reach an intersection. Hike straight on the 0.5-mile (0.8-km) Emery Path, which rises aggressively through narrow gaps in the ledge and up a rugged

Owl fledglings guard the Hemlock Trail.

landscape with the assistance of well-constructed rock steps. Beyond the midway point, the Homans Path enters from the right. Stay left and ascend past a series of pleasant vistas before leveling off at a three-way junction.

Join the 1-mile (1.6-km) Schiff Path leading right. The first half of this scenic route gains modest elevation with minor ups and a few downs. At first the forest comprises an assortment of northern hardwoods but becomes dominated by evergreens as the trail surface transitions to exposed ledge. The canopy also thins and affords impressive viewpoints east over The Tarn to Champlain Mountain's rugged slopes.

As the Dorr Mountain Ladder Trail converges from the left, follow the Schiff Path as it swings sharply west to begin the second half of its journey. Climbing more aggressively, each step up the granite terrain leads to even more expansive views of surrounding mountains and valleys. The incline eases as you arrive at a four-way intersection.

Turn left and follow the Dorr Mountain South Ridge Trail 0.1-mile (0.2 km) to the 1270-foot (387-m) summit. The barren high point has a large cairn and ample places to grab a seat. Enjoy the breathtaking scenery, including Cadillac Mountain rising to the west and the coastal panorama south between Great Head and Otter Cove. Be sure to gaze up and look for turkey vultures soaring effortlessly in the mountain air.

Retrace your steps to the four-way intersection and proceed straight on the Dorr Mountain North Ridge Trail. This 0.8-mile (1.3-km) route begins easily across mostly open terrain, with splendid views across Frenchman Bay to Schoodic and Black Mountains rising in the distance. Carefully descend the granite slope in and out of the pine forest. As the angle becomes steeper, the footing can be tricky if the ground is wet or icy. After dropping into the trees for good, the trail remains steep but easier to navigate.

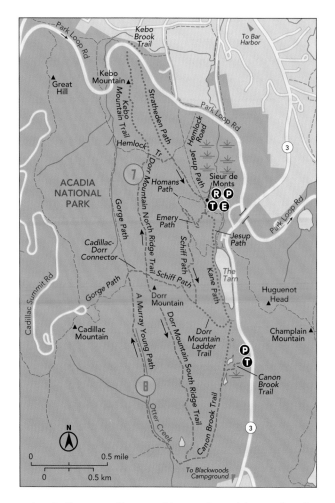

Level off at a confluence of four paths and bear right. The well-used Hemlock Trail descends rapidly 0.2 mile (0.3 km). Paralleling a seasonal stream, the route becomes easier with each step before ending at Hemlock Road. Stay right and follow this wide corridor 0.4 mile (0.6 km) back to Sieur de Monts.

GOING FARTHER

Complete a more rigorous 6-mile (9.7-km) traverse of Dorr Mountain's entire ridge by combining this hike with portions of Hikes 6, 8, and 9. Begin in the low country on the Jesup Path, Kane Path, and Canon Brook Trail. Scramble up Dorr Mountain's South Ridge, down the North Ridge, and over Kebo Mountain. Use the Kebo Brook Trail, Stratheden Path, and Hemlock Road to complete the challenging but rewarding circuit.

8   DORR MOUNTAIN SOUTH RIDGE

Distance: 4.8-mile (7.7-km) loop
Elevation gain: 1300 feet (400 m)
High point: 1270 feet (387 m)
Difficulty: Challenging
Trail surface: Granite ledges, bog bridging, rock steps, and uneven terrain
Map: Park brochure
GPS: 44.348241°N, 68.202072°W
Notes: Traffic moves quickly past parking area

Cadillac Mountain towers over Dorr Mountain's summit cairn.

> Combining one of the mountain's more popular trails with a less-traveled route, this challenging circuit offers rewards ranging from awe-inspiring vistas to serene mountain streams, and for those willing to look and listen, diverse signs of wild flora and fauna throughout.

GETTING THERE

From the Bar Harbor Village Green at the intersection of Mount Desert Street and Main Street, follow Route 3 (Main Street) south. Drive 3 miles (4.8 km) to the trailhead and parking on the right (just off the road).

ON THE TRAIL

The Canon Brook Trail, Dorr Mountain's most gradual approach, gently descends west from the parking area 0.3 mile (0.5 km) to start. As it reaches a sprawling wetland complex and a junction with the Kane Path, look for beaver dams, lodges, and chewed-up trees. The wetlands also attract many avian species, including eastern phoebes, tree swallows, and other birds that catch insects in midair.

Remain on the Canon Brook Trail as it bears sharply left. Over the next 0.7 mile (1.1 km) the well-used route meanders over the lightly rolling landscape. Continue under the shady canopy of northern hardwoods before swinging right and abruptly rising to the start of the Dorr Mountain South Ridge Trail. You will explore this path later; for now, stay straight on the Canon Brook Trail.

Descend easily around ledges, past cedar trees, and across an intermittent stream to reach the banks of Otter Creek in 0.2 mile (0.3 km). The Canon Brook Trail bears left and crosses the running water. Instead, join the A. Murray Young Path as it departs right. This secluded route, named in honor of a summer resident who left his mark on the island's trails during the park's formative years, winds up the valley following the shrinking stream. The trail uses well-placed stones and rock steps to ease the way. After climbing past a narrow gorge on the right, the footing becomes a bit rougher and more challenging. Take your time and before long the 1.1-mile (1.8-km) path leads to ocean views before ending in a narrow col separating Dorr and Cadillac Mountains.

The Gorge Path departs left toward Cadillac Mountain. A few steps ahead, at a second intersection, turn right onto the Cadillac-Dorr Connector. This 0.2-mile (0.3-km) trail wastes little time ascending Dorr Mountain. Large boulders turn to steep granite ledges as the first of many viewpoints emerges. The incline moderates at a four-way intersection. Bear right and follow the Dorr Mountain South Ridge Trail. It leads easily 0.1 mile (0.2 km) to the 1270-foot (387-m) summit.

The mountain's 360-degree views are a fitting tribute to George Dorr, whose foresight and actions in the early twentieth century were instrumental in the creation of the park enjoyed by so many today. Take in picturesque scenes in all directions of mountains, islands, distant peninsulas, and the Gulf of Maine's alluring waters. Cadillac Mountain's eastern slopes are especially impressive from this perspective.

Descend south from the summit cairn. The mountain's South Ridge Trail winds 1.3 miles (2.1 km) down from the peak. Weave along the smooth rock surface to multiple vistas showcasing the surrounding beauty. Just beyond the halfway point, the footing becomes steeper and rougher. Use caution, especially if it is wet or icy. After entering the forest for good, reach the Canon Brook Trail. Turn left and retrace your steps to the start.

OTHER OPTIONS

Consider a shorter but more challenging loop by ascending the Dorr Mountain Ladder Trail (dogs prohibited). Near the start, turn right onto the Kane Path and hike 0.3 mile (0.5 km) to reach this more intense route. Not a great option for those fearful of heights, the trail rises 0.4 mile (0.6 km) up ladders, through narrow gaps, and past stunning viewpoints before ending at the Schiff Path. Turn left to reach Dorr Mountain in 0.6 mile (1 km) and then descend the South Ridge Trail to complete a 3.9-mile (6.3-km) circuit.

SIEUR DE MONTS

Acadia's most influential founder George Dorr developed Sieur de Monts Spring as a welcome center in 1909 while the effort to build a park grew. Today, it houses the original Abbe Museum, a nature center, and the Wild Gardens of Acadia. Many hikes in this section begin at Sieur de Monts. Before hitting any of these trails consider exploring the museum, nature center, or the garden paths, which showcase the park's native plants.

9 SIEUR DE MONTS TO JORDAN POND

Distance: 5.4 miles (8.7 km)
Elevation gain: 1250 feet (380 m)
High point: 990 feet (302 m)
Difficulty: Challenging
Trail surface: Granite ledges, rock steps, crushed stone, and uneven terrain
Map: Park brochure
GPS: 44.362694°N, 68.207685°W
Notes: Requires Island Explorer; dogs not recommended; swimming in Jordan Pond prohibited; restrooms at both trailheads

Bookended by two of the park's most-frequented locations, this journey connecting them uses some of Acadia's less-traveled corridors while visiting wildlife-rich wetlands, cascading streams, picturesque ledges, and hidden forests.

GETTING THERE

From late June to mid-October, take an Island Explorer bus to Sieur de Monts. Buses stop at this trailhead throughout the day. After hiking to Jordan Pond House, grab an Island Explorer bus to get back to your car.

ON THE TRAIL

Hike past the nature center to reach the Jesup Path. Turn left onto this well-manicured trail. It crosses a service road, enters the forest, and winds gently 0.3 mile (0.5 km) to a major intersection near the Cromwell Brook headwaters.

Continue straight on the Kane Path as it parallels the western shore of The Tarn, a large, shallow pond slowly transitioning into a meadow. The route swings through boulders and hugs the water's edge, but the footing quickly improves. Remain on the Kane Path through a four-way trail junction and reach the Canon Brook Trail in 0.8 mile (1.3 km).

The surrounding wetland habitat is home to beaver, waterfowl, and other wildlife. Look for these critters as you follow the Canon Brook Trail south through the dense hardwood forest. The route has minor elevation change before rising to a junction with the Dorr Mountain South Ridge Trail in 0.7 mile (1.1 km).

Stay straight on the Canon Brook Trail and descend gently past small ledges to the banks of Otter Creek in 0.2 mile (0.3 km). At an intersection where the A. Murray Young Path departs right, cross the bubbling stream to the left. The Canon Brook Trail is about to get a lot more challenging.

Ascend the uneven terrain to a steep slope where rock steps head up this lightly used trail. Beside a small stream, the path's steps transition to granite ledges as the slope steepens. During the spring or after a shower, the footing can be tricky. However, wetter conditions also mean more impressive cascades as the running water careens through small flumes and gorges. The trail features some pleasant

Western vista from the Canon Brook Trail, near the Featherbed

vistas and then eases before reaching a trail junction 0.7 mile (1.1 km) from Otter Creek.

Head across the Cadillac South Ridge Trail as the Canon Brook Trail winds around the northern shore of the Feather-bed. Beyond this tiny seasonal pond lies an impressive ledge offering the day's most sweeping views. Check out Pemetic Mountain across the valley as well as distant scenes of rocky shoreline and islands trailing to the horizon.

Over the next 0.6 mile (1 km), the Canon Brook Trail drops steadily over rugged terrain. Take your time descending through this quiet corner of the park. It is an ideal locale to slow down and enjoy the area's rock formations, shrouded in carpets of wildflowers, ferns, and mosses. Level off near a secluded pond before rising to a three-way junction.

Turn left onto the Bubble and Jordan Ponds Path. With modest elevation change, it parallels a carriage road 0.4 mile (0.6 km) before crossing it. Remain on this pleasant for-ested route 1.1 miles (1.8 km) farther. Along the journey, hike straight through three trail junctions and safely cross Park Loop Road. A final descent ends at Jordan Pond.

Turn left onto the popular Jordan Pond Path and hike 0.4 mile (0.6 km) west along the scenic shoreline. Photo opportunities abound, including impressive views of Jordan Cliff

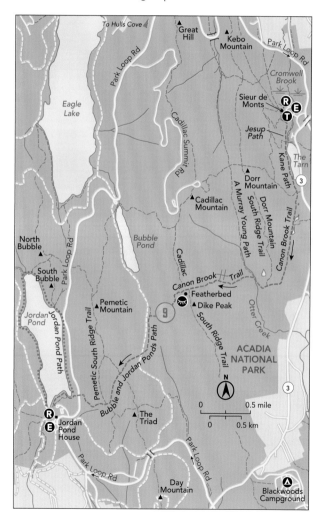

and the Bubbles. As you approach the pond's outlet stream, turn left onto the path heading to the Jordan Pond House (see "Jordan Pond House" sidebar in the Jordan Pond chapter). This is a great place to lounge before grabbing an Island Explorer bus to complete the day's journey.

GOING FARTHER

Upon reaching Jordan Pond, turn right to go the long way around the stunning body of water on the Jordan Pond Path (see Hike 15). Adding this mostly flat loop results in an 8.1-mile (13-km) hike.

10 CADILLAC MOUNTAIN NORTH RIDGE

Distance: 5-mile (8-km) loop
Elevation gain: 1400 feet (430 m)
High point: 1530 feet (466 m)
Difficulty: Challenging
Trail surface: Granite ledges, rock steps, and uneven terrain
Map: Park brochure
GPS: 44.378467°N, 68.229612°W
Notes: Restroom at the summit

> While Cadillac features many trail options, this one combines the best of what the mountain offers, including a long, scenic ridgeline, a deep, glacier-carved gorge, small cascades, and an occasional scramble up the park's ubiquitous granite slopes.

GETTING THERE

Driving: From the Hulls Cove Visitor Center, follow signs pointing to Park Loop Road and drive south 3 miles (4.8 km) to a three-way intersection. Turn left onto the one-way road leading toward Sand Beach. Drive 0.3 mile (0.5 km) to the

Hikers enjoy views of Frenchman Bay from the Cadillac North Ridge Trail.

Cadillac North Ridge parking on the left. Because parking is limited, the transit option, when available, is the best choice.

Transit: From late June to mid-October, Island Explorer buses stop at this popular trailhead throughout the day. Note: The Cadillac North Ridge bus stop and the trailhead parking are in different places. From the bus stop, the Kebo Brook Trail leads 0.1 mile (0.2 km) east to the parking area and trailhead.

ON THE TRAIL

From the parking area, do not cross the road. Instead, find the Kebo Brook Trail at the lot's western edge. Descend the staircase to a three-way junction. If using the Island Explorer, reach this same junction by hiking from the bus stop, located 0.1 mile (0.2 km) west.

Follow the Kebo Brook Trail as it descends gradually east 0.4 mile (0.6 km). Bear right on the Gorge Path and rise gently 0.4 mile (0.6 km) to the banks of Kebo Brook, where the trail heads under a historic stone bridge and beneath Park Loop Road.

Ascend a staircase to the right and proceed 0.4 mile (0.6 km) across mostly level terrain to a junction with the Hemlock Trail. Remain on the Gorge Path as it parallels the shrinking brook, occasionally crossing it. The footing can be a bit slippery, but the trail is adorned with many rock steps to aid passage. The climb intensifies and enters a chasm between rock walls, then climbs steeply out of the shady gorge. The surrounding dense evergreen forest is the perfect place to listen for the flutelike call of the winter wren—a diminutive bird that is difficult to see but often heard.

One mile (1.6 km) from the Hemlock Trail junction, arrive in the narrow saddle between Dorr and Cadillac Mountains. Turn right at the saddle's second junction, remaining on the Gorge Path. The final 0.4-mile (0.6-km), 500-foot (150-m) ascent begins with a short scramble up a steep rocky slope. With each step, the scenery becomes more impressive and the incline less pronounced.

Before long, reach the summit area's sounds and crowds. For an informative tour, follow the 0.3-mile (0.5-km) loop trail that circles the open ledges. Please remain on the hardened surface to protect the mountain's vegetation. The path culminates with breathtaking views atop a promontory slightly lower than the less scenic 1530-foot (466-m) summit—0.1 mile (0.2 km) west on the South Ridge Trail.

Find the North Ridge Trail. It departs right, where the summit road exits the parking area. The upper portion of this 2.2-mile (3.5-km) route remains almost entirely in the open. Although it is well blazed, many unmarked paths diverge in multiple directions. Take your time; the route quickly becomes easier to follow. On clear days, the horizon seems endless across Frenchman Bay to distant interior hills and mountains.

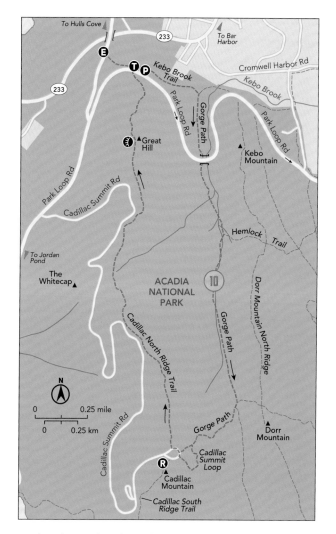

After descending through the barren landscape, approach the summit road in 0.7 mile (1.1 km). The trail drops into the forest before emerging from the trees once again as it approaches the pavement a last time in 0.5 mile (0.8 km). Watch your footing over the final 1 mile (1.6 km) as you make your way to Great Hill, a final bump on the ridge. Here semi-open ledges offer one last vista.

Carefully proceed down a final pitch to the parking area. To grab an Island Explorer bus, take the staircase to the Kebo Brook Trail. Turn left and hike 0.1 mile (0.2 km) to the bus stop.

11   CADILLAC MOUNTAIN WEST FACE

Distance: 4.7-mile (7.6-km) loop
Elevation gain: 1325 feet (405 m)
High point: 1530 feet (466 m)
Difficulty: Challenging
Trail surface: Granite ledges, crushed stone, and uneven terrain
Map: Park brochure
GPS: 44.349962°N, 68.241516°W
Notes: Restroom at the summit; not recommended for dogs

> Offering rewards around every bend, this extremely challenging loop ascends the most difficult option to the top of Cadillac, traverses a high, scenic ridgeline, and descends the mountain's quietest path before concluding across inviting terrain.

GETTING THERE

Driving: From the Hulls Cove Visitor Center, follow signs pointing to Park Loop Road and drive south 3 miles (4.8 km) to a three-way intersection. Continue straight on Park Loop Road and drive 1.9 miles (3 km) to the Bubble Pond parking area on the left. Note that parking here is prohibited when Island Explorer buses are operating between late June and mid-October.

HOW CADILLAC MOUNTAIN GOT ITS NAME

As French settlers looked to Maine in the late seventeenth century, Antoine Laumet headed from the motherland to America. In 1688, he assumed the title Sieur de la Mothe Cadillac and soon was granted a hundred thousand acres of the Maine coast, including all of Mount Desert Island. His dreams of a feudal estate did not last long. He and his wife left and headed west for new opportunities. Credited with founding the city of Detroit, Cadillac's name has survived there in the automobile industry and in Maine atop Acadia's highest summit.

Transit: From late June to mid-October, Island Explorer buses stop at this trailhead throughout the day.

ON THE TRAIL

Head to Bubble Pond's scenic shore and the start of the 0.9-mile (1.4-km) Cadillac West Face Trail. The park's most difficult non-ladder route, especially when wet, the trail wastes little time scaling the precipitous slope. Loose rocks transition to granite ledges as the canopy thins. As you head east, enjoy ever-increasing views of Bubble Pond far below and Pemetic Mountain across the valley.

Beyond the midway point, the trail swings right. Although climbing less aggressively, it skirts the steep slope at a difficult angle. Take your time and make your way to a more open and forgiving landscape. Surrounded by breathtaking scenery, rise to the Cadillac South Ridge Trail.

The hike will eventually follow the route right, but first turn left to reach the mountain's summit area in 0.5 mile (0.8 km). There are stunning views west to Sargent Mountain and beyond as you head across the open terrain. After

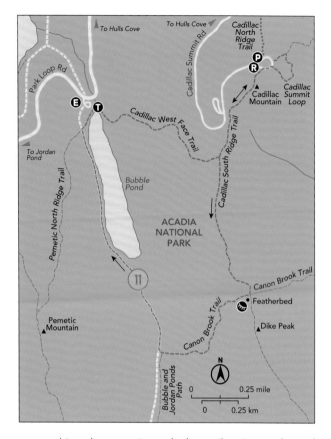

approaching the summit road, the trail swings right and enters the boreal forest. Head over a wooded knob, drop to a service road, and then ascend to the mountain's 1530-foot (466-m) high point.

Continue 0.1 mile (0.2 km) to the trail's end. Turn right and hike around the parking lot to the wide-open summit area. Although slightly lower than the top, this spot showcases more expansive views. Explore the 0.3-mile (0.5-km) paved loop trail that winds around the barren landscape. Signs point out features in sight on clear days. Please stay on the trail to protect fragile vegetation and be prepared for a lot of company.

Retrace your steps 0.5 mile (0.8 km) along the South Ridge Trail, then continue straight another 0.7 mile (1.1 km) farther. In spots, the route is almost as forgiving as a paved sidewalk. With few trees around, the views are spectacular. A short, steady descent into the forest ends at a four-way intersection near the Featherbed, a small pond that is often dry late in the summer.

Follow the Canon Brook Trail right as it winds around the shore to a scenic ledge. This quiet corner of the mountain is a great place to enjoy the surrounding beauty, seemingly worlds away from the summit crowds. The Canon Brook Trail descends aggressively. Take your time to navigate the rock steps and uneven surfaces. Hike 0.6 mile (1 km) down to a small body of water and then ascend easily to a junction.

Turn right on the Bubble and Jordan Ponds Path, which soon ends at a carriage road. Bear right and follow this

Bubble Pond sits in a narrow gap between Cadillac and Pemetic Mountains.

multiuse corridor 1.1 miles (1.8 km) for the rest of the hike; after a modest descent, the road levels off along the shores of Bubble Pond, where you will enjoy splendid views of Cadillac Mountain's impressive western slopes until you are back to the starting point.

GOING FARTHER

If you are using the Island Explorer, consider reversing the described route and descending the Cadillac North Ridge Trail (Hike 10). Begin on the carriage road, then combine the Canon Brook, South Ridge, and North Ridge Trails to complete a 5.3-mile (8.5-km) hike. This option avoids the challenging Cadillac West Face Trail while connecting two Island Explorer bus stops.

12 CADILLAC MOUNTAIN SOUTH RIDGE

Distance: 7.4 miles (11.9 km)
Elevation gain: 1525 feet (465 m)
High point: 1530 feet (466 m)
Difficulty: Challenging
Trail surface: Granite ledges, bog bridging, and uneven terrain
Map: Park brochure
GPS: 44.312870°N, 68.214830°W
Notes: Restroom at the summit

The South Ridge Trail on a clear day features a seemingly endless series of breathtaking views, but do not underestimate the difficulty or exposure to the elements faced on the longest and most forgiving route to Cadillac's alluring summit.

GETTING THERE

From the Bar Harbor Village Green at the intersection of Mount Desert Street and Main Street, follow Route 3 (Main

Views are plentiful along the Cadillac South Ridge Trail.

Street) south. Drive 5.6 miles (9 km) to the trailhead (just beyond the Blackwoods Campground entrance). Parking is an option on both sides of the road.

ON THE TRAIL

On the road's north side, climb the rock steps to a kiosk and the start of the South Ridge Trail. This gradual ascent of Cadillac features three legs of similar lengths. The first segment begins in a dense evergreen forest where boardwalks occasionally provide relief from the root-covered ground. Enjoy the shade as you wind methodically along 1 mile (1.6 km) of modest elevation gain to a junction.

Turn right on the Eagles Crag Trail and scramble 0.2 mile (0.3 km) to an open ledge with pleasant views northeast to Champlain Mountain. Gazing north, catch the first glimpse of Cadillac's summit area—two-thirds of the ascent remains. The Eagles Crag Trail ends in 0.1 mile (0.2 km).

Bear right, rejoin the main route, and begin the trek's second leg. While this 1.1-mile (1.8-km) portion rises more aggressively than the first leg, the trail's granite surface provides better footing unless it is wet or icy. Wind your way through the thinning pine forest as more scenery comes into

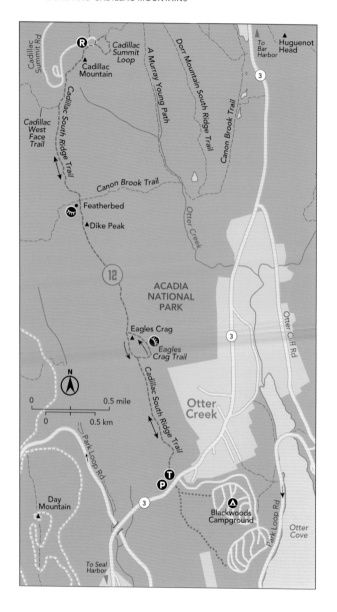

view, culminating with a 360-degree panorama atop 1073-foot (327-m) Dike Peak. Drop 0.1 mile (0.2 km) to reach a four-way junction. The Featherbed, a small seasonal pond, lies to the left. This small forested saddle on the ridge is a good place to grab a snack before tackling the final third of the ascent.

The South Ridge Trail leads you through an intersection with the Canon Brook Trail. Plod 0.1 mile (0.2 km) up the day's steepest climb. The route quickly moderates while traversing smooth, open ledges featuring views in all directions. Much of Mount Desert Island and surrounding lands are in view as you pass a junction with the Cadillac West Face Trail in 0.6 mile (1 km) and approach the summit road soon after.

The blue-blazed path swings right, heads over a forested knob, and then drops into a saddle. Cross a service road before arriving at the park's 1530-foot (466-m) high point. Mostly surrounded by trees, Cadillac's summit is not as popular as the slightly lower open area located 0.1 mile (0.2 km) ahead, just beyond the trail's end.

Before heading back down the South Ridge Trail, take time to explore the summit area. A 0.3-mile (0.5-km) loop offers information on the region and provides various perspectives of the mountains, islands, and bays in sight. Be prepared to share the experience with many others; some have hiked here, but most have not. On your return trek, retrace your steps throughout, with one exception. Upon reaching the Eagles Crag Trail, stay on the slightly more direct main trail that leads right.

OTHER OPTIONS

If staying overnight at Acadia's Blackwoods Campground, you can start this hike from your campsite. The South Ridge Trail begins at the campground, and depending on where your site is located, this will add as much as 1 mile (1.6 km) roundtrip to the day's journey.

JORDAN POND

Jordan Pond and nearby Eagle Lake lie in valleys carved by ice that receded thousands of years ago. Their pristine waters are surrounded by towering mountain slopes, thick forests, and stunning natural beauty. While this is the park's most inland section, breathtaking ocean views abound from atop the many open summits dotting the landscape.

The vast collection of hiking trails and carriage roads that traverse the lands surrounding Jordan Pond lure outdoor adventurers for casual jaunts, gradual climbs, and rigorous excursions. While routes to well-known destinations like Pemetic Mountain, the Bubbles, and Penobscot Mountain are quite popular, a few more off-the-beaten paths are also available for those seeking a bit of solitude at Conners Nubble or The Triad.

Parking is limited near Jordan Pond and at other nearby locations. For a less hectic experience, hop on an Island Explorer bus to access these well-used trailheads. And be sure to secure a reservation if you want to add the Jordan Pond House's famous popovers and tea to your day's hiking itinerary (see "Jordan Pond House" sidebar).

OPPOSITE: *Park visitors enjoy outdoor dining at Jordan Pond House.*

13 THE BUBBLES AND EAGLE LAKE

Distance: 4.2-mile (6.8-km) loop
Elevation gain: 1000 feet (300 m)
High point: 872 feet (266 m)
Difficulty: Moderate to challenging
Trail surface: Granite ledges, rock steps, bog bridging, and uneven terrain
Map: Park brochure
GPS: 44.341069°N, 68.250286°W
Notes: Swimming prohibited in lake; privy at trailhead

> Surrounded by Acadia's highest peaks and most sparkling lakes, this scenic loop travels to popular as well as not-so-crowded corners of the park on a photogenic journey through ever-changing terrain that offers numerous optional extensions and shortcuts.

GETTING THERE

Driving: From the Hulls Cove Visitor Center, follow signs pointing to Park Loop Road and drive south 3 miles (4.8 km) to a three-way intersection. Continue straight on Park Loop Road and head toward Jordan Pond. In 2.8 miles (4.5 km) turn right into the parking area. Because parking is limited, the transit option, when available, is the best choice.

Transit: From late June to mid-October, Island Explorer buses stop at this trailhead throughout the day

ON THE TRAIL

Head up the well-trodden Bubbles Divide Trail and reach a junction in 0.1 mile (0.2 km). Turn right onto the Jordan Pond Carry Trail and leave most of the crowds behind—for now. Descending gently 0.5 mile (0.8 km), this lesser-used route meanders through a dense forest before reaching a carriage road. Cross the multiuse corridor. On the other side, bog

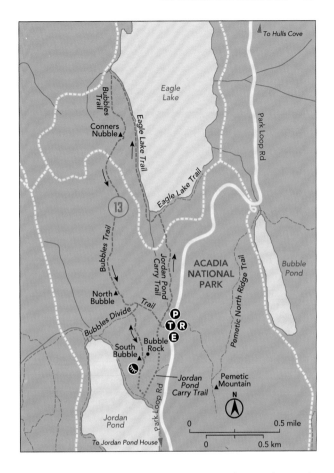

bridging and rock steps lead 0.1 mile (0.2 km) to the Eagle Lake Trail, where a short, unmarked spur provides access to the shoreline and views of the expansive waters.

Follow the Eagle Lake Trail left. The footing is good initially, but the route becomes increasingly rocky. Paralleling the shoreline for nearly a mile, it never strays far from the lake and showcases endless outlooks of Cadillac and

Cadillac Mountain and Eagle Lake from the Bubbles Trail

Pemetic Mountains. Once you are through an evergreen tunnel, a junction awaits.

Turn left on the Bubbles Trail and begin a steady 0.4-mile (0.6-km) climb under a thinning canopy of leaves to the wide-open summit of 588-foot (179-m) Conners Nubble. This infrequently visited peak showcases impressive views of the sprawling body of water below. Dropping very steeply southwest, the path leads immediately to a carriage road. On the opposite side, begin the 0.8-mile (1.3-km) ascent of the North Bubble ridgeline.

Once again, the path weaves through increasingly sparse vegetation as it scales a granite ledge to a dramatic clifftop with stunning views of nearby peaks as well as scenes northeast to Frenchman Bay. Following a brief drop, rise to the top of North Bubble, 2.9 miles (4.7 km) from the start. Standing 872 feet (266 m) above sea level, the mountain offers fine snapshot views of Jordan Pond far below and Sargent Mountain towering to the west.

Meandering southwest, the path descends rock and ledges 0.3 mile (0.5 km)—watch your step—to a junction with the popular Bubbles Divide Trail. Although the parking lot is to the left, before completing the journey, turn right—South Bubble and its famous rock are too alluring to skip.

The two routes coincide for less than 0.1 mile (0.2 km). Then, bear left onto the Bubbles Trail and follow the wide path 0.2 mile (0.3 km) to the 764-foot (233-m) summit. While lower than its neighbor to the north, South Bubble provides the day's most intimate views of sprawling Jordan Pond and the surrounding peaks if you continue south on the trail just beyond the high point. Also, be sure to follow the short spur to Bubble Rock, a large boulder miraculously balancing on the mountainside. A glacier deposited the impressive rock here many millennia ago.

Retrace your steps to the Bubbles Divide Trail and turn right. Enjoy the straightforward descent 0.4 mile (0.6 km) to the parking area. While the trail is modestly steep in places, the footing is good throughout.

OTHER OPTIONS

Complete the most-popular journey from this trailhead by limiting your exploration to North and South Bubbles. It is 1.6 miles (2.6 km) out and back using the Bubbles Divide and Bubbles Trails. Conversely, take the Jordan Pond Carry Trail south to Jordan Pond and the start of the Bubbles Trail. Scramble up South Bubble's steep slopes, proceed to North Bubble, and then head back to the start to complete an adventurous 1.8-mile (2.9-km) circuit.

14 DAY MOUNTAIN, THE TRIAD, AND PEMETIC MOUNTAIN

Distance: 6.8-mile (10.9-km) loop
Elevation gain: 1650 feet (505 m)
High point: 1248 feet (380 m)
Difficulty: Challenging
Trail surface: Granite ledges, crushed stone, bog bridging, and uneven terrain
Map: Park brochure
GPS: 44.299320°N, 68.227613°W
Notes: Hike begins on private property

> This challenging loop, with many options to shorten the adventure, traverses some of the park's quieter trails while offering breathtaking views, hidden vistas, and alluring geologic formations.

GETTING THERE

Driving: From the Bar Harbor Village Green, follow Route 3 south. In 5.6 miles (9 km), pass the Blackwoods Campground. Continue another 1.3 miles (2.1 km) to the parking area on the left.

Transit: From June to mid-October, Island Explorer buses pass this trailhead throughout the day. Since it is not a regular stop, inform the driver where you are going when entering the bus.

ON THE TRAIL

Carefully cross Route 3 to the trailhead, where a short path immediately leads right to a monument celebrating Samuel de Champlain's arrival to Mount Desert Island. The Day Mountain Trail heads across level terrain to an intersection of carriage roads in 0.2 mile (0.3 km). Proceed straight, briefly following the wider corridor leading to Day

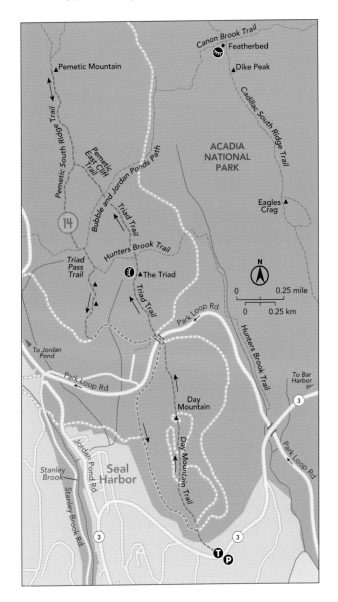

Cranberry Isles from the Hunters Brook Trail

Mountain, before veering left to rejoin the blue-blazed hiking trail.

Over the next 0.6 mile (1 km), gradually climb the rocky slopes and cross a carriage road three times—the third crossing is just before the 583-foot (180-m) summit. While partly forested, Day Mountain displays pleasant coastal scenery including the Cranberry Isles, Swans Island, Frenchboro, and Isle au Haut.

The Day Mountain Trail continues north 0.4 mile (0.6 km). It begins easily, crosses a carriage road, and descends steadily until it ends. Follow the carriage road straight across the stone bridge to the Triad Trail, where an aggressive 0.3-mile (0.5-km) ascent awaits. Scale rock and granite to reach The Triad's 698-foot (216-m) summit, where a perch features western views of rolling ridges.

The moss-lined Triad Trail proceeds north through a thick spruce forest. It crosses the Hunters Brook Trail in 0.1 mile (0.2 km) before arriving 0.4 mile (0.6 km) later at a four-way intersection. Hike straight onto the 0.3-mile (0.5-km) Pemetic

East Cliff Trail. Initially level, the terrain quickly intensifies. Wind through a boulder field, then scale the ledge-covered slopes. The incline eases and the trees grow sparser as you arrive at the Pemetic South Ridge Trail.

Bear right and head up the barren landscape. Though challenging, each step leads to more expansive views, culminating in 0.6 mile (1 km) atop 1248-foot (380-m) Pemetic Mountain. The summit's 360-degree panorama encompasses Cadillac and Sargent Mountains, Jordan Pond, the Bubbles, and dramatic ocean scenery.

Retrace your steps south, but at the East Cliff junction stay right, remaining on the Pemetic South Ridge Trail, which drops steadily another 0.6 mile (1 km). Take your time and listen for the gentle hammering of hairy woodpeckers foraging in the surrounding boreal landscape. When the trail ends, turn left and follow the Bubble and Jordan Ponds Path, which immediately leads to another intersection.

Swing right on the Triad Pass Trail and hike 0.2 mile (0.3 km). Turn right again, onto a 0.5-mile (0.8-km) segment of the Hunters Brook Trail. After ascending two bumps, this quiet route traverses an open ridge with breathtaking coastal views. A short, steep descent ensues—watch your footing, especially if the ground is wet. The trail ends at a cedar post at a carriage road.

Turn left and follow the carriage road. In 0.4 mile (0.6 km), bear right and recross the stone bridge over Park Loop Road. Rather than heading back over Day Mountain, stay right on the more inviting carriage road. The wide corridor leads 0.6 mile (1 km) to a junction. Continue straight another 0.8 mile (1.3 km), rising easily to the Day Mountain Trail. Turn right to complete your journey.

OTHER OPTIONS

Opportunities abound to shorten the hike by turning around at Day Mountain, The Triad, or the top of the Pemetic East

Cliff Trail. Roundtrip distance for these three destinations are 1.6 miles (2.6 km), 3.5 miles (5.6 km), and 5.8 miles (9.3 km), respectively.

15 JORDAN POND LOOP

Distance: 3.5-mile (5.6-km) loop
Elevation gain: 50 feet (15 m)
High point: 300 feet (91 m)
Difficulty: Easy to moderate
Trail surface: Crushed stone, bog bridging, and uneven terrain
Map: Park brochure
GPS: 44.320544°N, 68.253613°W
Notes: Swimming prohibited; restroom at trailhead

> In the heart of the park, this popular loop invites hikers of all ages to venture along its course and marvel at mountain reflections, serenading loons, colorful wildflowers, and boundless natural beauty.

GETTING THERE

Driving: From the Hulls Cove Visitor Center, follow signs pointing to Park Loop Road and drive south 3 miles (4.8 km) to a three-way intersection. Continue straight on Park Loop Road and drive south 4.4 miles (7.1 km) to the Jordan Pond parking area on the right. To park at this lot during peak times, you may need a reservation through www.recreation.gov.

Transit: From late June to mid-October, Island Explorer buses stop at this destination throughout the day.

ON THE TRAIL

The Island Explorer bus stop is in front of the Jordan Pond House. If arriving by car, walk 0.1 mile (0.2 km) west from the parking area to reach the building and begin the hike.

JORDAN POND HOUSE

Nellie McIntire began a restaurant and started serving popovers and tea in 1893 near the shores of Jordan Pond. This began what has become a more than century-long tradition for Acadia visitors, drawn for the food and the location's spectacular vista. While the original structure burned in 1979, the existing building replaced it in 1982. The Jordan Pond House is owned and operated by a private, authorized National Park Service concessioner. Open from late April through the end of October, this popular destination accepts reservations—especially recommended between 11:30 AM and 4:00 PM. Visit their website for more information (see Contact Information).

Depart the building's northern side and follow the trail leading to the shoreline, intersecting the Jordan Pond Path. From this spot, taking a photo of the Bubbles rising above the distant shore might be an unwritten requirement for all park visitors, but there will be many additional photogenic spots over the next 3.3 miles (5.3 km).

Turn left and follow the trail toward the pond's outlet stream. The Jordan Pond Path swings right onto a carriage road. After crossing the running water, bear right once again and join the level trail as it parallels the cedar-shaded shoreline. Much of the route is along wooden boardwalks that rise above the wet, rocky, rooted landscape. Enjoy the leisurely stroll, stopping at the many scenic vistas. In addition to the Bubbles, Pemetic Mountain dominates the backdrop.

In 1.5 miles (2.4 km) from the pond's outlet, the Deer Brook Trail departs left. The Jordan Pond Path transitions at this point, becoming a wider, crushed-stone corridor. Continue circling the pond in a clockwise direction, exit the forest, and cross two wooden bridges leading over incoming streams. Be alert for waterfowl feeding in the nearby waters. With luck, common mergansers will be present. The males of

The Bubbles are on display from many spots along the Jordan Pond Path.

this large duck species feature green heads, while those of females and young are rust colored.

In 0.2 mile (0.3 km), pass the base of the Bubbles Divide Trail, which scales a rockslide providing access to the popular, rounded peaks. Stay on the main trail and continue along the pond's edge, remaining mostly in the open. In 0.4 mile (0.6 km), arrive at an intersection where the Bubbles and Jordan Pond Carry Trails diverge left.

Remain straight on the Jordan Pond Path and begin a pleasant jaunt along the eastern shore. From numerous vantage points through the evergreens, the scenes of Jordan Cliff are dramatic. In 0.9 mile (1.4 km), reach a signpost where a trail heads left to Pemetic Mountain. Stay straight here for the final 0.3-mile (0.5-km) stretch, which swings right and crosses a bridge dividing the pond from a marshy cove. Hug the shoreline and once again enjoy incredible views of the Bubbles across the sprawling pond until completing the circuit.

GOING FARTHER

To briefly escape the crowds, take in some mountaintop views, and significantly rachet up the hike's difficulty, consider adding a 2.5-mile (4-km) extension using the Deer Brook,

Sargent East Face, Sargent South Ridge, and Penobscot Mountain Trails—small cascades and a high-elevation pond are added bonuses. You can also extend the hike 0.3 mile (0.5 km) by heading up the Bubbles Divide Trail, then following the Bubbles Trail up and over South Bubble. This challenging diversion omits a short portion of the Jordan Pond Path but features breathtaking views from South Bubble.

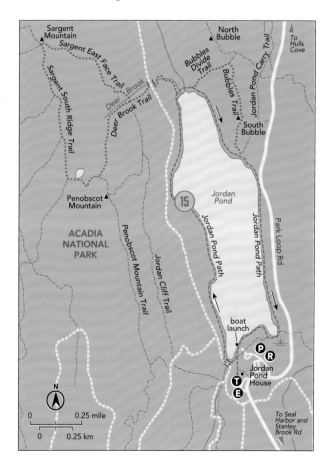

16 PEMETIC MOUNTAIN AND JORDAN POND

Distance: 4.2-mile (6.8-km) loop
Elevation gain: 1100 feet (335 m)
High point: 1248 feet (380 m)
Difficulty: Challenging
Trail surface: Crushed stone, rock steps, granite ledges, and uneven terrain
Map: Park brochure
GPS: 44.322273°N, 68.253034°W
Notes: Swimming prohibited; restroom at trailhead and en route

> Scaling the peak that bears the name used by Maine's Wabanaki to describe a place of "sloping land," this challenging loop combines jaw-dropping scenery atop barren granite ledges, subtle shoreline beauty, and hidden gems in between.

GETTING THERE

Driving: From the Hulls Cove Visitor Center, follow signs pointing to Park Loop Road and drive south 3 miles (4.8 km) to a three-way intersection. Continue straight on Park Loop Road and drive south 4.4 miles (7.1 km) to the Jordan Pond parking area on the right. To park at this lot during peak times, you may need a reservation through www.recreation.gov.

Transit: From late June to mid-October, Island Explorer buses stop at this destination throughout the day.

ON THE TRAIL

The Island Explorer bus stop is in front of the Jordan Pond House, and the parking area is 0.1 mile (0.2 km) to the east. From the parking area's northernmost loop, follow the wide path that leads straight to the pond's boat launch. If beginning at the Jordan Pond House, take the shortest route to

Taking a break to enjoy coastal views from Pemetic South Ridge Trail

the pond's shore and turn right to quickly reach the boat launch site.

From the boat launch, head east along the Jordan Pond Path. It parallels the water's edge, offering splendid views of the expansive body of water and the Bubbles, rising above the distant shore. In 0.2 mile (0.3 km), the well-manicured path crosses a small bridge dividing the pond from a more secluded marsh and immediately reaches a cedar post on the right for the Bubble and Jordan Ponds Path—the start of the loop.

Stay straight on the Jordan Pond Path. The wide route hugs the shoreline and traverses level terrain for 0.9 mile (1.4 km), providing a great opportunity to warm up the muscles in preparation for more challenging trails ahead. After crossing a small bridge, turn right onto the Jordan Pond Carry Trail. Shaded by northern hardwoods, this lightly used trail rises moderately. Continue straight where a path diverges right to Park Loop Road, and then arrive at a four-way intersection in 0.4 mile (0.6 km). Bear right on the Bubbles Divide Trail, which quickly leads to a parking area.

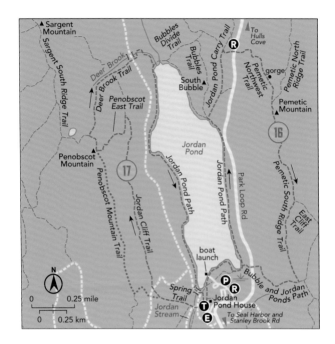

Carefully cross Park Loop Road to reach the Pemetic Northwest Trail. This 0.4-mile (0.6-km) route wastes little time plodding up the rocky landscape. Boulders turn to ledge as the incline steepens. Near the midway point two options are available, both difficult. To the left, a path parallels a small stream in a narrow chasm where wooden ladders assist the climb. The second option heads along the edge of the small gorge and ascends granite ledges through the thinning canopy. The routes soon converge, and shortly after the terrain eases at a junction with the Pemetic North Ridge Trail.

Stay right for the final 0.1-mile (0.2-km) stretch to the wide-open 1248-foot (380-m) summit. Once you are atop the rocky knob, find breathtaking views of Mount Desert Island in all directions. The views of Cadillac to the east, Sargent to the west, and the sprawling lakes below are most impressive.

Resume hiking along the Pemetic South Ridge Trail, which remains in the open for 0.6 mile (1 km). Take your time and enjoy the panoramic scenery; it is difficult to stop gazing at the coastline, islands, and bays. Stay right as the Pemetic East Cliff Trail diverges left and begin a 0.6-mile (1-km) mostly forested stretch. Down the steep slope, wind past rocks and across ledges with limited views through the spruce and fir forest. The South Ridge Trail eventually levels off, ending at an intersection.

Turn right onto the Bubble and Jordan Ponds Path and descend gradually 0.4 mile (0.6 km) to Park Loop Road. Proceed with caution and rejoin the trail on the other side. Descend 0.1 mile (0.2 km) to reach the Jordan Pond Path. Turn left and retrace your steps to the start.

17 PENOBSCOT MOUNTAIN AND JORDAN CLIFF

Distance: 4.2-mile (6.8-km) loop
Elevation gain: 1200 feet (365 m)
High point: 1181 feet (360 m)
Difficulty: Technical (nontechnical option)
Trail surface: Granite ledges, ladders, crushed stone, and uneven terrain
Map: Park brochure
GPS: 44.320544°N, 68.253613°W
Notes: Trail closes seasonally to protect nesting falcons (alternative route available) swimming prohibited in Jordan Pond; restroom at trailhead; dogs not permitted on Jordan Cliff Trail

This scenic loop explores one of the park's less-traveled technical trails showcasing exquisite views of Jordan Pond from

The Jordan Cliff Trail is appropriately named.

above, then completes the journey with more intimate perspectives along the shoreline.

GETTING THERE

Driving: From the Hulls Cove Visitor Center, follow signs pointing to Park Loop Road and drive south 3 miles (4.8 km) to a three-way intersection. Continue straight on Park Loop Road and drive south 4.4 miles (7.1 km) to the Jordan Pond parking area on the right. To park at this lot during peak times, you may need a reservation through www.recreation.gov.

Transit: From late June to mid-October, Island Explorer buses stop at this destination throughout the day.

ON THE TRAIL

The Island Explorer bus stop is in front of the Jordan Pond House. If arriving by car, walk 0.1 mile (0.2 km) from the parking area to reach the building. From the Jordan Pond House, descend west to a carriage road intersection. Follow the road straight toward Jordan Stream and then bear right at a cedar post pointing toward Penobscot and Sargent Mountains.

After crossing the wooden bridge, stay right on the Spring Trail. It rises gently 0.3 mile (0.5 km) to the start of the Jordan Cliff Trail. If ladders and steep drop-offs are not your pleasure, or if the route is closed because of nesting peregrine falcons, take the Spring Trail left to reach the Penobscot Mountain summit (see Other Options). Otherwise, turn right onto the more adventurous route.

Cross a carriage road and begin a steady climb up a narrowing ridge. At first, the Jordan Cliff Trail ascends a mostly forested landscape. The path wraps around the ledge-covered slope and requires an occasional descent, including one that leads down a narrow wooden staircase.

The trail's second half is dominated by scree slopes, narrow shelves atop granite ledges, and iron rungs leading up steep inclines. It is not the place to be if you are afraid of heights or the footing is wet. Be sure to take plenty of breaks to marvel at the mesmerizing views of Jordan Pond, the Bubbles, and Pemetic Mountain. Use extreme caution across the many sharp drop-offs.

After hiking 1.2 miles (1.9 km) along the Jordan Cliff Trail, turn left onto the Penobscot East Trail. This route is equally scenic but scrambles less precariously up the mountain's rocky surface. In and out of the stunted evergreen forest, wind 0.4 mile (0.6 km) to Penobscot Mountain's treeless summit. Enjoy stunning scenery in all directions from atop this 1181-foot (360-m) peak.

Follow the Penobscot Mountain Trail north toward Sargent Mountain and proceed cautiously down the rocky surface. Hike 0.1 mile (0.2 km) to a three-way intersection and then turn right onto the Deer Brook Trail. While this route drops nearly 800 feet (245 m) in 0.7 mile (1.1 km), the footing is mostly forgiving. Follow the trail through a four-way intersection, past a small cascade, across a carriage road, and down to the shores of Jordan Pond.

At the water's edge, turn right onto the Jordan Pond Path. The mostly level trail hugs the shoreline for much of its 1.4-mile (2.3-km) journey, usually with the aid of bog bridging. Take advantage of the scenic spots along the way while looking for black-capped chickadees, golden-crowned kinglets, and red-breasted nuthatches foraging in the cedar-dominated forest. The trail eventually leads to a carriage road. Turn left on the multiuse corridor, cross the outlet stream, and then immediately turn left again to reach one last view from the shores of Jordan Pond. Head 0.1 mile (0.2 km) south, away from the water's edge, to complete the hike at the Jordan Pond House (see sidebar in Hike 15).

OTHER OPTIONS

Avoid Jordan Cliff by remaining on the Spring Trail, which uses rock steps to aggressively climb 0.2 mile (0.3 km) to the Penobscot Mountain Trail. Follow this path right. It rises 1 mile (1.6 km) across wide-open terrain to the Penobscot Mountain summit. Continue the described route from here to complete a 3.8-mile (6.1-km) loop.

NORTHEAST HARBOR

Northeast Harbor is dominated by Sargent Mountain, the second-highest summit in Acadia. This section of the park also features many minor rocky peaks, sprawling granite ridges, dense evergreen forests, cascading streams, and scenic ponds. Located in the heart of Mount Desert Island, this region's open summits offer the most comprehensive views of the park.

Northeast Harbor is a hiker's paradise, with a menu of trails and carriage roads that provide a multitude of options. Although many routes are popular, the ambiance here is more low key than at destinations located farther east along Park Loop Road. In addition, this region offers the best opportunity for longer treks, especially with the use of Island Explorer buses.

Trailheads along a well-used state highway provide access to the region's paths. Touring the Land & Garden Preserve's nearby Asticou Azalea and Thuya Gardens is a pleasant addition to a glorious day of hiking, as is grabbing a passenger ferry to the park's Islesford Historical Museum on Little Cranberry Island.

OPPOSITE: *Bald Peak dominates views from Upper Hadlock Pond (Hike 19).*

18 PENOBSCOT AND SARGENT MOUNTAINS

Distance: 8 miles (12.9 km)
Elevation gain: 1750 feet (535 m)
High point: 1373 feet (419 m)
Difficulty: Challenging
Trail surface: Crushed stone, granite ledges, rock steps, and uneven terrain
Map: Park brochure
GPS: 44.312269°N, 68.285407°W
Notes: Described route requires Island Explorer; see alternative below

> Through quiet forests, across breathtaking ridgelines, along remote streams, this challenging excursion follows a journey less traveled to two of the park's most-visited summits.

GETTING THERE

Driving: From the junction of Routes 102 and 3/198 in Somesville, follow Route 3/198 toward Northeast Harbor. Drive 5.1 miles (8.2 km) to the Brown Mountain parking area on the left.

Transit: From late June to mid-October, take an Island Explorer bus to Brown Mountain to start the hike and pick up the bus at Jordan Pond at the end for the return.

ON THE TRAIL

Find the trailhead at the parking area's eastern edge. The hike follows carriage roads to start. Rise gently and stay right at two three-way intersections. Then, follow the carriage road until reaching the Sargent South Ridge Trail, 0.7 mile (1.1 km) from the start. Follow this route right as it drops 0.1 mile (0.2 km).

The Penobscot Mountain Trail traverses wide-open granite ledges.

Turn left onto the Asticou and Jordan Pond Path as it parallels the boundary of the Land & Garden Preserve (see "Land & Garden Preserve" sidebar) and reaches a junction in 0.2 mile (0.3 km). Stay left on the main trail. It descends north, crosses Little Harbor Brook, passes through a stand of impressive white pines, and reaches an intersection in 0.5 mile (0.8 km).

Bear left on the Penobscot Mountain Trail and climb moderately 0.2 mile (0.3 km), while crossing three carriage roads. A more aggressive climb soon ensues. Wind up around rocks and ledges to the first of many vistas. The path moderates through the thinning forest as the Spring Trail enters from the right in 0.8 mile (1.3 km).

The final 1-mile (1.6-km) stretch north to Penobscot Mountain's summit is almost entirely in the open. Take your time and follow the cairns that weave up the ridge. With each step, more expansive views emerge of Jordan Pond, the rocky coastline, and higher peaks, including Cadillac Mountain. Once atop the 1181-foot (360-m) high point, enjoy a 360-degree panorama.

The Penobscot Mountain Trail continues north from the summit. Watch your step down the steep slope that leads 0.1 mile (0.2 km) into a saddle. Stay straight at a junction where the Deer Brook Trail departs right. The path cuts through fern-draped boulders, heads over a small knob, and then descends to Sargent Mountain Pond. Use designated spots to view the water in order to protect this diminutive, high-elevation pond. A steep 0.1-mile (0.2-km) climb ends at a junction.

Follow the well-used Sargent South Ridge Trail right and hike 0.7 mile (1.1 km) to the 1373-foot (419-m) summit. Although occasionally surrounded by trees and fragile plants, the trail mostly traverses barren ledges. Sargent's oft-windy high point features sweeping views in all directions, encompassing most of Mount Desert Island and many inland features as well.

Retrace your steps to the Penobscot Mountain Trail, then stay right on the Sargent South Ridge Trail. It descends steadily atop exposed granite. Take your time and enjoy the picturesque coastal scenery in the distance before arriving at a four-way intersection in 0.5 mile (0.8 km).

Turn left onto the Amphitheater Trail, a secluded path that drops rapidly into a deep, carved-out valley. Level off in 0.3 mile (0.5 km) near Little Harbor Brook. Over the next 0.8 mile (1.3 km), the path remains close to the small, cascading stream, crossing it repeatedly. Near the trail's halfway point, rock steps lead under an immense stone bridge. The route's uneven footing slowly eases as the nearby brook gets larger.

At the trail's end, turn left and follow the carriage road 0.3 mile (0.5 km). After crossing the Penobscot Mountain Trail, bear left to rejoin the Asticou and Jordan Pond Path. This well-manicured route is the perfect way to end the day's challenging adventure, crossing carriage roads at the beginning and end of the journey. With modest elevation change, hike 1 mile (1.6 km) to the Jordan Pond House, where you can relax, have a small bite to eat (reservations recommended),

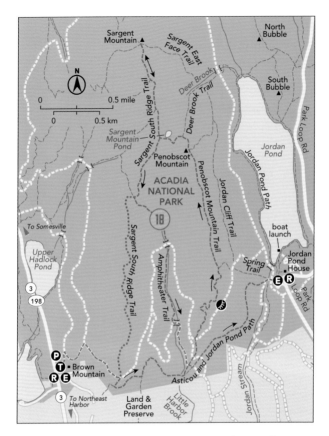

and take in the surrounding beauty (see "Jordan Pond House" sidebar in the Jordan Pond chapter). Return to your vehicle via an Island Explorer bus.

OTHER OPTIONS

If the Island Explorer is not available or convenient, there are two good options beginning and ending at the Brown Mountain Trailhead. Near the end of the described route, retrace your steps west along the Asticou and Jordan Pond Path.

This adds 0.6 mile (1 km) to the hike. Alternatively, descend the Sargent South Ridge Trail, rather than the Amphitheater Trail, to complete an 8-mile (12.9-km) journey.

LAND & GARDEN PRESERVE

Begun by David and Peggy Rockefeller, the Land & Garden Preserve is a membership-based organization that manages more than 1400 acres (567 hectares) of gardens and wildlands on Acadia's boundary near Northeast Harbor. Many visitors are drawn to the historic Asticou Azalea and Thuya Gardens that the preserve manages. In addition, hikers are invited to explore peaceful footpaths leading to Eliot Mountain, along Little Harbor Brook, and around Little Long Pond. The preserve's network seamlessly connects to the park's trails south of Jordan Pond and Penobscot Mountain.

19 NORUMBEGA MOUNTAIN AND HADLOCK PONDS

Distance: 3.8-mile (6.1-km) loop
Elevation gain: 800 feet (245 m)
High point: 846 feet (258 m)
Difficulty: Moderate to challenging
Trail surface: Granite ledges, rock steps, bog bridging, and uneven terrain
Map: Park brochure
GPS: 44.325796°N, 68.291353°W
Notes: Swimming in ponds prohibited

This circuit along the banks of scenic ponds and above the eastern shore of Somes Sound is challenging at first, but much of the journey offers easy to moderate terrain on trails less traveled in a busy corner of the park.

GETTING THERE

Driving: From the junction of Routes 102 and 3/198 in Somesville, follow Route 3/198 toward Northeast Harbor. Drive 4.1 miles (6.6 km) to the parking area on the right.

Transit: From late June to mid-October, Island Explorer buses pass this trailhead throughout the day. Since it is not a regular stop, inform the driver where you are going when entering the bus.

Coastal views from the Norumbega Mountain Trail

ON THE TRAIL

Just north of the parking area, head up the Goat Trail as it enters the forest and immediately reaches a junction. Stay straight on the Goat Trail and proceed up the steep slope. While numerous rock steps and short switchbacks ease the

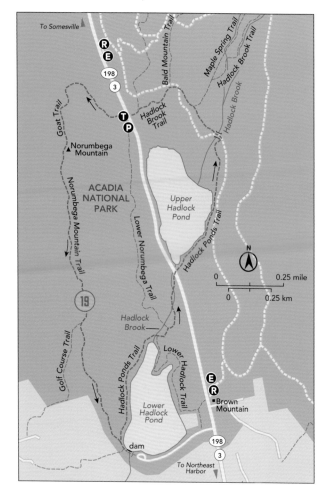

way, the challenging route quickly gets the blood flowing. In 0.4 mile (0.6 km), emerge onto semi-open ledges and enjoy photo-worthy views east to Sargent Mountain. Swing south and ascend gradually 0.2 mile (0.3 km) to the 846-foot (258-m) summit.

Named for a fabled city of riches that French explorer Samuel de Champlain searched for in the early sixteenth century, Norumbega Mountain offers limited views from its pine-forested high point. However, hike south along the Norumbega Mountain Trail where more panoramas await. To the west, enjoy scenes of Acadia Mountain and Southwest Harbor as you slowly descend 0.8 mile (1.3 km). Stay straight at a junction where the Golf Course Trail departs right, then drop more rapidly into the thicker evergreen forest. In 0.6 mile (1 km), reach an intersection with the Hadlock Ponds Trail.

The loop continues left, but first walk a few dozen steps ahead to a small dam on the shores of Lower Hadlock Pond. Swimming is prohibited in this public water supply but photographing the blue waters and surrounding peaks is not. The pond is also a great place to spot common loons surfacing time and again after feeding beneath the water's surface. With a little luck, one may show off its haunting call.

Return to the Hadlock Ponds Trail and turn right. With little elevation change, the trail hugs the pond's scenic western shoreline for 0.5 mile (0.8 km) until you reach a junction with the Lower Hadlock Trail, entering from the right. Continue straight and parallel Hadlock Brook another 0.1 mile (0.2 km) to a junction with the Lower Norumbega Trail. This 0.9-mile (1.4-km) path departs left and offers a slightly shorter alternative route back. To complete a more scenic circuit, stay right on the Hadlock Ponds Trail. The footing is initially rough but quickly leads to bog bridging that winds to Route 3/198 in 0.2 mile (0.3 km).

Safely cross the busy highway and rejoin the trail as it leads along Upper Hadlock Pond's southeastern shore. Over the next 0.3 mile (0.5 km) enjoy intimate views of the sprawling wetland and Bald Peak rising high above it to the north. Boardwalks keep your feet high and dry. After leaving the picturesque pond behind, hike 0.2 mile (0.3 km) to a carriage road. Follow this wide corridor left over a small stone bridge and then bear right back onto the Hadlock Ponds Trail.

The forested path rises gently 0.2 mile (0.3 km) before ending. Turn left onto the Hadlock Brook Trail for the final 0.3-mile (0.5-km) leg of the journey. After descending the ledge-covered slope, recross the carriage road. Hike straight through two intersections and ascend easily to the trailhead. Use caution crossing the often busy road to reach the parking area.

20 BALD PEAK AND PARKMAN MOUNTAIN

Distance: **2.7-mile (4.3-km) loop**
Elevation gain: **900 feet (275 m)**
High point: **974 feet (297 m)**
Difficulty: **Moderate to challenging**
Trail surface: **Rocks, granite ledges, and uneven terrain**
Map: **Park brochure**
GPS: **44.325796°N, 68.291353°W**
Notes: **Not recommended when wet**

> Rewards come early and often along this loop where steep scrambles up glacier-sculpted granite ledges lead to sweeping panoramas atop lower peaks on the western slopes of Sargent Mountain.

GETTING THERE
Driving: From the junction of Routes 102 and 3/198 in Somesville, follow Route 3/198 toward Northeast Harbor. Drive 4.1 miles (6.6 km) to the parking area on the right.

Enjoy views of Norumbega Mountain and Upper Hadlock Pond from the Parkman Mountain Trail.

Transit: From late June to mid-October, Island Explorer buses pass this trailhead throughout the day. Since it is not a regular stop, inform the driver where you are going when entering the bus.

ON THE TRAIL

Carefully cross the pavement to reach the cedar post marking the start of the Hadlock Brook Trail. Enter the dark boreal forest and immediately reach the Parkman Mountain Trail on your left; you will return via this route. Continue straight on the Hadlock Brook Trail. The path descends easily 0.2 mile (0.3 km) to a small stream and trail junction.

Turn left on the Bald Mountain Trail, which soon crosses a carriage road before returning to the forest. Follow the narrow route as it parallels the bubbling stream 0.2 mile (0.3 km) to a second carriage road crossing. Catch your breath; the degree of difficulty is about to ratchet up a few notches.

Rise aggressively up the rocky slope. In 0.1 mile (0.2 km), the trail descends into a small saddle. This short reprieve is

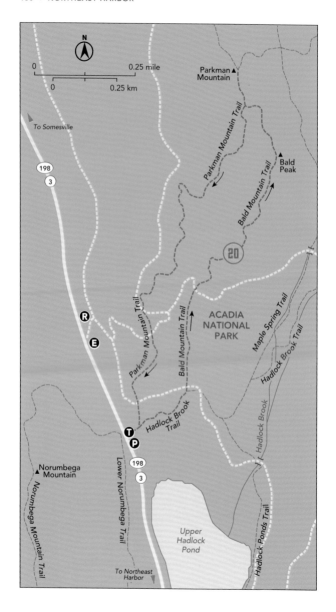

immediately followed by the day's most challenging incline. While the 0.4-mile (0.6-km) ascent is intense, it traverses wide-open granite ledges affording breathtaking views across Upper Hadlock Pond and over Northeast Harbor to islands fading into the distance. If the rocks are slick, watch your footing as you make your way to Bald Peak's 974-foot (297-m) high point. Once atop the barren summit, enjoy views in all directions, including of Sargent Mountain towering to the east and Somes Sound's upper reaches lying to the northwest.

The loop continues north 0.2 mile (0.3 km) along the Bald Mountain Trail. Take your time to successfully navigate the ledge-covered route into a secluded col, then rise quickly to a junction with the Parkman Mountain Trail. The way back heads left, but for now turn right to scale the trail's namesake peak in 0.1 mile (0.2 km). A bit lower than its neighbor, Parkman's 941-foot (287-m) treeless summit offers similar scenery from a slightly different perspective.

Begin the 1.5-mile (2.4-km) descent by retracing your steps to the Bald Mountain Trail intersection and then stay right on the Parkman Mountain Trail. Over the next mile (1.6 km), the scenic path meanders across open ledges, down a few steep pitches, and through the spruce-dominated forest before reaching the first of three carriage road crossings. Descend quickly to cross the other two and in 0.4 mile (0.6 km) arrive at a junction with the Hadlock Brook Trail. Turn right to complete the hike.

21 SARGENT MOUNTAIN AND HADLOCK BROOK

Distance: 4.2-mile (6.8-km) loop
Elevation gain: 1200 feet (365 m)
High point: 1373 feet (419 m)
Difficulty: Challenging

Trail surface: Granite ledges and uneven terrain
Map: Park brochure
GPS: 44.325796°N, 68.291353°W
Notes: Good winter route after snowstorm

This gradual, forested approach to the park's highest road-less summit and surrounding barren ridgeline invites exploration throughout the year, combining breathtaking mountain vistas with serene, cascading streams.

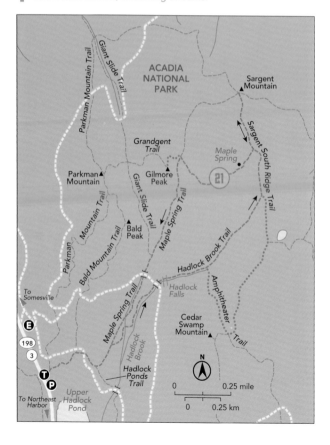

GETTING THERE

Driving: From the junction of Routes 102 and 3/198 in Somesville, follow Route 3/198 toward Northeast Harbor. Drive 4.1 miles (6.6 km) to the parking area on the right.

Transit: From late June to mid-October, Island Explorer buses pass this trailhead throughout the day. Since it is not a regular stop, inform the driver where you are going when entering the bus.

ON THE TRAIL

Carefully cross the pavement to reach the Hadlock Brook Trailhead on the east side of the busy road. Gently descend into a dense stand of spruce trees while passing trails leading left to Parkman and Bald Mountains before reaching a carriage road 0.2 mile (0.3 km) from the start.

The path resumes on the opposite side of the wide corridor and scales the ledge-covered slope. In 0.1 mile (0.2 km), swing left and level off as the Hadlock Ponds Trail enters from the right. Continue another 0.1 mile (0.2 km) over lightly rolling terrain to a fork in the trail—the start of the day's loop.

Follow the Hadlock Brook Trail right. It soon crosses one branch of Hadlock Brook before paralleling another. Heading up the forested slope, the route approaches a carriage road in 0.4 mile (0.6 km) and offers two options: To the right, the path winds under a large stone bridge to the base of Hadlock Falls, which can be very impressive during spring or after a storm. A more straightforward option leads left and crosses the carriage road above the bridge. The two quickly rejoin.

Ascend more steadily while following the shrinking brook higher up the mountain. Stay left at a junction with the Amphitheater Trail in 0.3 mile (0.5 km). Before long, the final 0.5-mile (0.8-km) stretch slowly emerges onto a series of open ledges. Enjoy the expanding western vistas while rising to a junction with the Sargent South Ridge Trail.

Windswept snow covers the Sargent South Ridge Trail.

The open landscape provides views in all directions. During winter months, the surrounding granite and stunted evergreen trees offer desirable habitat for snowy owls. These white, diurnal birds of prey blend in well with snow, but with a little patience you may be able to spot one on the hunt. Please enjoy from a distance.

Turn left and follow the trail as it gradually ascends 0.5 mile (0.8 km) to the mountain's wide-open 1373-foot (419-m) high point. Pay close attention to the cairns that mark the winding route and avoid shortcuts to minimize impacts to the fragile plants that abound. With scenery in all directions and fewer crowds than on its taller neighbor to the east, Sargent is the park's most inviting mountaintop.

Retrace your steps 0.3 mile (0.5 km) along the Sargent South Ridge Trail, then turn right onto the Maple Spring Trail. Over the next 0.5 mile (0.8 km), the path winds past its namesake natural feature, ascends a small unnamed bump, and descends rapidly to a four-way intersection with the Grandgent Trail.

Stay left on the Maple Spring Trail and watch your step while descending into the narrowing valley. The alluring path follows a bubbling branch of Hadlock Brook that generates soothing sounds as it cascades over rocks, flows around boulders, and winds between small ledges. In 0.5 mile (0.8 km), hike straight at a junction with the Giant Slide Trail.

The route leads 0.1 mile (0.2 km) farther before heading under an impressive stone bridge. The Maple Spring Trail's final 0.3-mile (0.5-km) stretch moderates with each step. Veer right and retrace your steps 0.4 mile (0.6 km) along the Hadlock Brook Trail to complete the hike.

GOING FARTHER

Complete a more challenging 4.9-mile (7.9-km) circuit by making two adjustments. During the ascent, turn right and follow the Amphitheater Trail 0.3 mile (0.5 km). Then hike 1.2 miles (1.9 km) north along the Sargent South Ridge Trail to reach the summit. On the descent, add a 0.2-mile (0.3-km) roundtrip diversion along the Grandgent Trail to enjoy Gilmore Peak's wide-open high point.

OTHER OPTIONS

After a healthy rainstorm or on rainy days, consider a 1.6-mile (2.6-km) roundtrip trek to Hadlock Falls. The nearby carriage roads also provide good opportunities to expand your exploration, allowing you to avoid slippery hiking trails.

22 SARGENT MOUNTAIN AND GIANT SLIDE

Distance: **4.6-mile (7.4-km) loop**
Elevation gain: **1400 feet (430 m)**
High point: **1373 feet (419 m)**
Difficulty: **Challenging**

Trail surface: Rock steps, granite ledges, bog bridging, and uneven terrain
Map: Park brochure
GPS: 44.350178°N, 68.301913°W
Notes: Trail begins on private property

> One of the quieter approaches to Sargent Mountain, this very challenging loop carves through narrow passageways, around boulders, and alongside a bubbling stream before traversing steep, open granite ledges showcasing panoramic views in all directions.

GETTING THERE

Driving: From the junction of Routes 102 and 3/198 in Somesville, follow Route 3/198 toward Northeast Harbor. Drive 2.4 miles (3.9 km) to the trailhead on the left. There are ample spaces to parallel park along either side of the road.

Transit: From June to mid-October, Island Explorer buses pass this popular trailhead throughout the day. Since it is not a regular stop, inform the driver where you are going when entering the bus.

ON THE TRAIL

The Giant Slide Trail begins on private property with a conservation easement that allows public access. Please respect the landowner's privacy and remain on the trail as it winds across bog bridging to the base of a granite ledge draped in fragile mosses and lichens. Head up and over the small bump and in 0.4 mile (0.6 km) enter the park. The route continues easily another 0.2 mile (0.3 km) to a carriage road.

After crossing the wide multiuse corridor, the trail rises more steadily and approaches Sargent Brook. Parallel the small stream into the deepening valley. As the Giant Slide's obstacles block the way, follow the blue-blazed path around boulders, through tight squeezes, and up the rugged terrain.

A young hiker heads up the Giant Slide Trail.

Take your time; the footing can be challenging, especially when the trail is wet. Reach a four-way intersection 1.1 miles (1.8 km) from the trailhead—the loop begins here.

Plod straight ahead on the Giant Slide Trail as it tunnels through a tiny cave. The persistent route snakes its way up the secluded gorge 0.2 mile (0.3 km) before traversing the brook one last time. Much easier terrain follows. Cross a carriage road before reaching a confluence of trails in 0.4 mile (0.6 km).

Turn left onto the Grandgent Trail. While this path is not as rough as the Giant Slide, the angle of the slope is a lot more daunting. Catch your breath before scrambling 0.2 mile

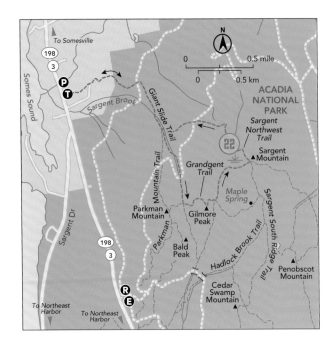

(0.3 km) to Gilmore Peak's 1036-foot (316-m) summit. From this barren pinnacle there are exquisite views south to the ocean and west over Somes Sound.

The Grandgent Trail continues north and then east, quickly descending 0.1 mile (0.2 km). Stay left on the Grandgent Trail at a four-way junction. The climb's final 0.5-mile (0.8-km) portion begins gradually, but not for long. Carefully scale the steep slopes through the thinning canopy of trees. The Grandgent Trail ends atop Sargent Mountain's 1373-foot (419-m) high point, which is near the center of Mount Desert Island. Few places provide more extensive views of the park.

Head down the Sargent Northwest Trail, a route that leaves the summit in the appropriate direction. This 1-mile (1.6-km) path descends at a steady pace throughout. Take your time and partake of the many vistas, especially along the trail's upper reaches. The sparsely forested terrain is also a good location to spot white-throated sparrows and hear their distinctive *Old Sam Peabody, Peabody* call—an enduring sound of summer in Maine.

In 0.7 mile (1.1 km), cross a carriage road, then drop rapidly 0.3 mile (0.5 km). Safely cross Sargent Brook to reach the Giant Slide Trail. Turn right to retrace your steps 1.1 miles (1.8 km) to the trailhead. Use extra care; this trail is more difficult on the descent and with tired legs.

23   SARGENT MOUNTAIN TRAVERSE

Distance: 6.1 miles (9.8 km)
Elevation gain: 1600 feet (490 m)
High point: 1373 feet (419 m)
Difficulty: Challenging
Trail surface: Rocks, granite ledges, and uneven terrain
Map: Park brochure
GPS: 44.329478°N, 68.293075°W
Notes: Requires Island Explorer; privies at both trailheads

> The benefit of taking the Island Explorer is your ability to begin and end at distant trailheads such as this Sargent Mountain Traverse, which combines four barren summits, a glorious ridge walk, and seemingly endless panoramic vistas.

GETTING THERE
From late June to mid-October, take an Island Explorer bus to the Parkman Mountain stop to start the hike and pick up a bus at the Brown Mountain stop at the end for the return.

ON THE TRAIL
Look for the kiosk near the bus stop marking the entrance to the carriage road. The hike will begin and end on these

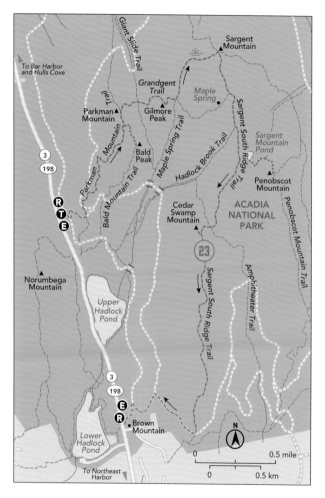

multiuse corridors. Follow trail etiquette by using the right-hand side of the path and allowing bicyclists, equestrians, and others to pass safely.

Beyond a gate, follow the carriage road right and almost immediately reach an intersection. Veer left and wind gently up the slope to an intersection with the Parkman Mountain Trail. Join this narrower hiking route as it enters the forest to the left. It climbs quickly before crossing another carriage road.

The Parkman Mountain Trail begins a steady 1.1-mile (1.8-km) ascent that includes a handful of more challenging sections. Watch your step as you head up the increasingly rocky slopes. The surrounding forest thins and the views become more extensive with higher elevation. Stay straight as the Bald Mountain Trail enters from the right. A final scramble leads to Parkman's 941-foot (287-m) summit and spectacular 360-degree scenery.

Heading east off the summit, join the 1.3-mile (2.1-km) Grandgent Trail to reach the trek's next two peaks. The first half of the route descends swiftly into a boreal forest draped in boulders, heads straight through a four-way junction with the Giant Slide Trail, and then rises aggressively to the 1036-foot (316-m) mostly treeless summit of Gilmore Peak. To complete the trail's second half, drop rapidly to a four-way junction. Stay left on the Grandgent Trail and hike past a small wetland before tackling a more daunting incline over open ledges to the large cairn atop Sargent Mountain's barren high point at 1373 feet (419 m). This is the perfect place to gaze upon the islands, inlets, mountains, and bays in all directions.

Continue the adventure along the mountain's South Ridge Trail, one of the park's most inviting routes. At first the elevation changes very little across an open expanse that often captures the shadows of the long, soaring wingspans of bald eagles. These majestic symbols of the nation have made an incredible comeback in recent decades and are commonly spotted throughout the park.

Hike straight, passing junctions with the Maple Spring and Hadlock Brook Trails diverging right.

In 0.8 mile (1.3 km), continue right at a junction where the Penobscot Mountain Trail leads left. The Sargent South

Gilmore Peak features pleasant western views.

Ridge Trail becomes a little more challenging over the next 0.5 mile (0.8 km), but it remains as beautiful. The rocky path makes its way around the upper reaches of the Amphitheater, a wide bowl that descends south toward the ocean.

At a four-way intersection, continue straight on the Sargent South Ridge Trail. A short drop into a narrow notch is followed by a 0.1-mile (0.2-km) climb to the Cedar Swamp Mountain spur on the right. This short, mostly level side trail leads to the day's fourth and final pinnacle, a 942-foot (287-m) peak that provides a great perspective on the day's previously visited summits.

Return to the main trail and bear right. The final 1.3 miles (2.1 km) along the ridge features a few minor ups. These obstacles break up an otherwise mostly gradual and pleasant descent.

Upon arriving at the carriage road, turn right and hike 0.4 mile (0.6 km) along the multiuse trail. Stay left at an intersection of carriage roads and do the same 0.2 mile (0.3 km) farther. When in doubt, follow the signs that point toward

Brown Mountain Gate. Find the Island Explorer bus stop in the parking lot to catch a ride back to your starting point.

GOING FARTHER

Add two wide-open summits to the excursion by visiting Bald Peak, a 0.4-mile (0.6-km) roundtrip extension, just before reaching Parkman Mountain. Then, after leaving Sargent Mountain, take a detour past Sargent Mountain Pond to Penobscot Mountain, a 0.6-mile (1-km) roundtrip diversion. These two options also add 350 feet (110 m) to the hike's elevation gain.

SOUTHWEST HARBOR

Southwest Harbor lies south of an alluring freshwater lake and at the mouth of a deep coastal inlet forming the only fjord-like body of water on America's Atlantic coast. These two signature natural features, Echo Lake and Somes Sound, are bordered by steep granite slopes and rocky promontories showcasing breathtaking views of sights both near and far.

Although home to some of Acadia's lower summits, the short paths that weave through this corner of the park are more challenging than you might expect. And since there are only a handful of trails available to visit such attractive locales as Flying Mountain, Beech Cliff, Valley Peak, and Acadia Mountain, you should also expect company on your travels.

While parking lots fill quickly and overflow spots are limited, Island Explorer buses serve the region's two most-popular trailheads. Get an early start to complete multiple hikes during the day or arrive later in the afternoon for a little solitude. When your hiking adventure is complete, cool off in Echo Lake (see "Echo Lake" sidebar in Hike 26) or take a stroll through nearby Somesville.

OPPOSITE: *Echo Lake lies far below Beech Cliff (Hike 26).*

24 ACADIA AND SAINT SAUVEUR MOUNTAINS

Distance: 4.9-mile (7.9-km) loop
Elevation gain: 1400 feet (430 m)
High point: 690 feet (210 m)
Difficulty: Challenging
Trail surface: Rock steps, granite ledges, and uneven terrain
Map: Park brochure
GPS: 44.321710°N, 68.332854°W
Notes: Privy at the trailhead

Featuring the island's only prominent east–west ridgeline, Acadia Mountain is the signature destination along this challenging circuit featuring awe-inspiring vantage points high above Somes Sound to loftier peaks and distant shorelines.

GETTING THERE

Driving: From the Somesville Fire Station, follow Route 102 south toward Southwest Harbor. Drive 2.5 miles (4 km) to the parking area on the right.

Transit: From June to mid-October, Island Explorer buses stop at this popular trailhead throughout the day.

ON THE TRAIL

If you have parked in the parking area, carefully cross the busy road and then head up a stone staircase to a kiosk. Turn left and follow the unmarked path that parallels Route 102 a short distance to the bus stop.

Take the wide Man O'War Brook Trail, which leads 0.1 mile (0.2 km) to a four-way intersection. Bear left on the Acadia Mountain Trail and begin a steady, sometimes steep, 0.6-mile (1-km) ascent. Walk over roots and scale ledges as the well-used path eventually reaches a handful of viewpoints. A final

Cranberry Isles from the Valley Peak Trail

climb leads to Acadia Mountain's 681-foot (207-m) rocky summit and panoramic views in most directions.

Continue east and weave through the thin pine-dominated forest. In 0.3 mile (0.5 km), the route swings south and heads down an increasingly steep slope. Watch your step on the exposed granite surface—the footing can be tricky when dry and is even more difficult if wet. Although challenging, the 0.7-mile (1.1-km) descent features incredible vistas of Somes Sound far below.

As you approach the salt water, the trail levels off, crosses Man O'War Brook, and arrives at a spur departing left. Follow this path 0.1 mile (0.2 km) down to an intimate outlook on the shoreline of the only fjord-like body of water on America's Atlantic coast. Carved by glaciers during the last ice age, its deepest point is more than 150 feet (46 m) below sea level.

Return to the main trail, turn left, and hike 0.1 mile (0.2 km) to a four-way intersection. To the right, the Man O'War Brook Trail leads 1 mile (1.6 km) back to the start—a good option to shorten the journey. Otherwise, head straight to enjoy rugged beauty along the Valley Peak Trail (not the Valley Cove Trail, which heads left).

The path gradually begins a 0.8-mile (1.3-km) climb. However, near the halfway point the terrain becomes steep and rugged. Ascend granite ledges featuring views to the east, culminating at a trail junction with a spectacular panorama, including Somes Sound, Sargent Mountain to the northeast, and the Cranberry Isles to the southeast.

A shortcut to Saint Sauveur Mountain leaves right, but you want to stay on the Valley Peak Trail. It descends gradually 0.3 mile (0.5 km) before rising to the top of a prominent ledge. Perched high above Flying Mountain, 505-foot (154-m) Valley Peak is the day's last scenic vantage point.

At a three-way intersection, just beyond the top of Valley Peak, turn right on the Saint Sauveur Trail and climb easily 0.5 mile (0.8 km) to the trail's namesake summit. The 690-foot (210-m) peak's dense evergreen forest blocks all views but attracts golden-crowned and ruby-crowned kinglets, diminutive, gregarious birds more often heard than seen. Patiently listen for their high-pitched calls.

The route continues north 0.3 mile (0.5 km) to a junction with the Ledge Trail. Remain on the Saint Sauveur Trail along its final 1-mile (1.6-km) stretch. Slithering across the rolling, rocky landscape, the route crosses one pine-covered ledge with limited views before dropping steadily. Make your way back to the Man O'War Brook Trail, 0.2 mile (0.3 km) after passing a path that departs left, leading more directly to the parking area. Turn left on the Man O'War Brook Trail to reach the bus stop.

OTHER OPTIONS

A good alternative to complete a shorter 2.7-mile (4.3-km) hike is to combine the Man O'War Brook and Acadia Mountain Trails. Consider doing this shorter loop in a

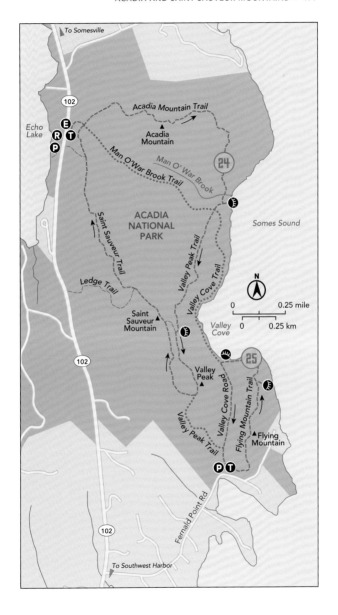

counterclockwise direction to ascend, rather than descend, the steepest section of the route.

25 FLYING MOUNTAIN

Distance: 1.5-mile (2.4-km) loop
Elevation gain: 350 feet (110 m)
High point: 284 feet (87 m)
Difficulty: Easy to moderate
Trail surface: Crushed stone, granite ledges, and uneven terrain
Map: Park brochure
GPS: 44.299631°N, 68.316335°W
Notes: Small, busy parking area

> This diminutive summit, which to the Wabanaki appeared to have flown off nearby Acadia Mountain, lures visitors of all ages with intimate views of Somes Sound, Valley Cove, and the area's more imposing peaks.

GETTING THERE

From the Somesville Fire Station, follow Route 102 south toward Southwest Harbor. Drive 4.5 miles (7.2 km) and then turn left onto Fernald Point Road. Continue 0.9 mile (1.4 km) to the parking area on the left. Limited parking is also available along the road.

ON THE TRAIL

From the parking area's east side, the Flying Mountain Trail rises steadily. At first the footing is easy, but the path soon scrambles up granite ledges to reach Flying Mountain's 284-foot (87-m) summit in 0.3 mile (0.5 km). Enjoy pleasant views south across the mouth of Somes Sound, recently reclassified by geologists as a fjard rather than a fjord. Its

Somes Sound from an outlook on the Flying Mountain Trail

slopes are not steep enough and its entrance not deep enough to meet the definition of its former classification.

A short, steep drop from the summit is followed by a 0.3-mile (0.5-km) stretch of rolling ridgeline. Meandering north with only modest elevation changes, the route soon arrives at a short spur leading right. Follow this path to an outlook high above the sound. There are impressive views across the deep salt water to Norumbega Mountain.

The main trail heads down a series of switchbacks, carving a course through the rocky terrain. Level off and parallel the shoreline as you travel west. Although it may be tempting to head to the water's edge, remain on the trail. The path quickly arrives at a wooden bridge. To the right, an official access route leads a few dozen steps to Valley Cove. Draped in scree slopes, this secluded shoreline was once used by British warships as shelter. Nearby Man O'War Brook served as a source of fresh water.

From the wooden bridge, the Flying Mountain Trail quickly ends at a three-way junction. Turn left onto Valley Cove Road, a wide corridor that leads 0.5 mile (0.8 km) south to the parking area. It is mostly level and an easy final leg of the circuit.

GOING FARTHER

From the end of the Flying Mountain Trail, turn right onto the Valley Cove Trail (often closed from April through early August to protect nesting peregrine falcons). Follow this difficult but scenic path 1.1 miles (1.8 km) and then turn left onto the Valley Peak Trail. Hike this 1.5-mile (2.4-km) route as it steeply climbs to a series of panoramic vistas before descending left to Valley Cove Road. Bear right for the final 0.1 mile (0.2 km) and complete a 3.8-mile (6.1-km) loop.

26 BEECH CLIFF AND BEECH MOUNTAIN

Distance: 3.1-mile (5-km) loop
Elevation gain: 900 feet (275 m)
High point: 841 feet (256 m)
Difficulty: Technical (nontechnical option)
Trail surface: Rock steps, granite ledge, ladders, bog bridging, and uneven terrain
Map: Park brochure
GPS: 44.314827°N, 68.336743°W
Notes: Restroom at trailhead and privy on hike; dogs prohibited on the Beech Cliff Trail

With steep ladders to start, followed by less strenuous terrain, this loop offers countless scenic vistas of surrounding peaks, nearby lakes, distant islands, and skies frequented by migrating raptors as cool fall breezes fill the air.

GETTING THERE

Driving: From the Somesville Fire Station, drive 3.3 miles (5.3 km) south on Route 102 toward Southwest Harbor. Turn right onto Echo Lake Beach Road. Stay right in 0.3 mile (0.5 km) and continue 0.2 mile (0.3 km) to the parking area.

Transit: From late June to mid-October, Island Explorer buses stop at this trailhead throughout the day.

ON THE TRAIL

Constructed by the Civilian Conservation Corps in the 1930s, the 0.5-mile (0.8-km) Beech Cliff Trail starts in a cul-de-sac at the parking area's north end. As the path reaches the bottom of the steep slope, swing left and ascend a rock staircase. In 0.2 mile (0.3 km), a spur departs right to a ledge with views of Echo Lake. The main route continues 0.3 mile (0.5 km) up seemingly impenetrable terrain. Weave under precipitous ledges and carefully ascend long metal ladders. The final pitch leads to a granite plateau with exhilarating views.

ECHO LAKE

Although most freshwater lakes and ponds on Mount Desert Island are closed to swimming, Echo Lake is one exception. Lifeguards staff a beach on its southern shores, an inviting place for park visitors to cool off on hot days, especially those Acadian travelers unwilling to brave Sand Beach's colder ocean waters. Parking is limited at this popular destination, but Island Explorer buses stop here throughout the day.

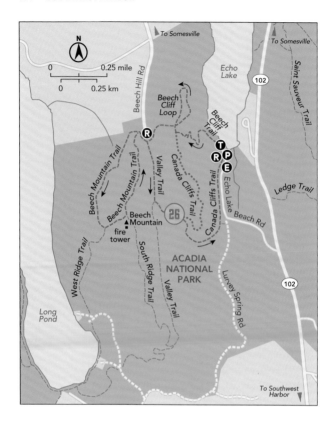

Turn right to reach the beginning of the 0.4-mile (0.6-km) Beech Cliff Loop. Hike the loop in a counterclockwise direction; the trail hugs the edge for 0.2 mile (0.3 km) while passing numerous spectacular vantage points of Echo Lake and some of the park's highest peaks to the east. The circuit winds up granite ledges before descending south to the main trail.

Bear right and walk 0.2 mile (0.3 km) down the well-manicured path to a parking area on the southern end of Beech Hill Road. Across the parking area, the Beech Mountain Trail departs just left of the privy. It quickly offers two

Long Pond and Blue Hill Bay from the Beech Mountain Trail

options. Follow the longer, more scenic 0.6-mile (1-km) western branch, which diverges to the right. Near this route's halfway point, the trail emerges from the forest, offering exceptional panoramas of Long Pond, Mansell Mountain, and Blue Hill Bay.

Back in the shade of evergreens, stay left at the West Ridge Trail intersection and proceed 0.1 mile (0.2 km) to a three-way junction. Scale the path that leads right to Beech Mountain's 841-foot (256-m) summit ledges and fine views in most directions. The mountain's fire tower is usually closed, but you can climb its stairs to take in more extensive scenery.

Return to the Beech Mountain Trail and turn right onto its eastern branch. Watch your footing as you hike 0.4 mile (0.6 km) down the rocky, uneven path. Upon returning to the Beech Hill Road parking area, head southeast along the pavement to find the Valley Trail.

Using an old woods road, this wide path drops easily 0.2 mile (0.3 km) to a junction. Turn left on the Canada Cliffs Trail and descend 0.2 mile (0.3 km) across the boggy landscape to a three-way junction (all three are branches of the Canada Cliffs Trail). Follow the path right. This final 0.6-mile

(1-km) leg of the journey parallels a small stream to start before heading down the steep mountain slope. Level off and hike north. After a short path leaves right to Lurvey Spring Road, continue straight, paralleling the pavement to the southern end of the Echo Lake parking area.

GOING FARTHER

If the Beech Cliff Trail's ladders are too intimidating or you are hiking with a dog, begin and end the hike using the Canada Cliffs Trail. From the southern end of the Echo Lake parking area, follow the Canada Cliffs Trail 0.6 mile (1 km) to its three-way intersection. Turn right and rise past numerous scenic outcrops. Pick up the described hike at the Beech Cliff Trail junction to complete a 3.7-mile (6-km) adventure.

OTHER OPTIONS

Although parking is limited, many begin at the Beech Mountain Trailhead. From this starting point, explore the 1-mile (1.6-km) Beech Mountain Trail loop, complete the 0.8-mile (1.3-km) jaunt of the Beech Cliff Loop, or hike both. The parking area is located at the southern end of Beech Hill Road, which leaves from Pretty Marsh Road 0.3 mile (0.5 km) west of the Somesville Fire Station.

27 BEECH MOUNTAIN SOUTH

Distance: 2.4-mile (3.9-km) loop
Elevation gain: 800 feet (245 m)
High point: 841 feet (256 m)
Difficulty: Moderate to challenging
Trail surface: Crushed stone, granite ledges, and uneven terrain
Map: Park brochure
GPS: 44.300225°N, 68.350068°W
Notes: Swimming prohibited in Long Pond

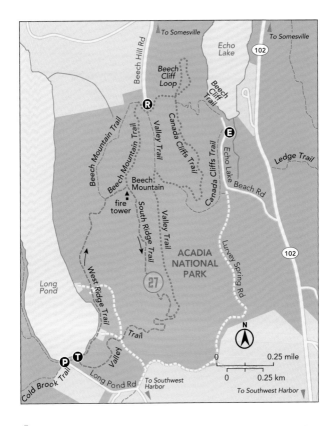

Explore Beech Mountain's quieter side on trails, where colorful songbirds provide welcome company near the shores of Long Pond and captivating scenery of Mount Desert Island's western side is showcased from ridgeline outlooks.

GETTING THERE

From the Somesville Fire Station, follow Route 102 south toward Southwest Harbor. Drive 4.8 miles (7.7 km) and turn right onto Seal Cove Road. Bear right on Long Pond Road in 0.6 mile (1 km) and then drive 1.2 miles (1.9 km) to the

Beech Mountain fire tower

trailhead. Find parking near the pond's shore and additional spots just before.

ON THE TRAIL

Start on the West Ridge Trail, which parallels Long Pond's southeastern shore. Enjoy the gentle terrain and remain on the blue-blazed path as it leads past a handful of private properties. In 0.3 mile (0.5 km), cross a dirt road and prepare for more challenging conditions.

The ensuing 0.5-mile (0.8-km) ascent is gradual and straightforward at first, but quickly changes. As you plod up the steep slope, the hardwood trees transition to pines and coarse soils become exposed granite. Through the widening gaps in the trees there are splendid photo-worthy views of Long Pond and Mansell Mountain's rugged slopes.

At the intersection with the Beech Mountain Trail, turn right and follow this well-used path 0.1 mile (0.2 km) to a spot just below the summit. Swing right, onto the South Ridge Trail, and scramble up smooth ledges to the base of a large fire tower.

The top of the summit's historic structure is usually closed, but you can scale some stairs for more extensive views. Built in 1962 to replace a wooden 1941 Civilian Conservation Corps–constructed tower, today's metal building defers to modern technology that can detect fires more effectively. Plenty of other spots atop the mostly open 841-foot (256-m) peak offer opportunities to enjoy scenes east to Acadia and Sargent Mountains and southwest across the string of islands leading to Isle au Haut.

Resume your hike by descending south off the summit along the 0.8-mile (1.3-km) South Ridge Trail. This attractive route weaves through pockets of boreal forests with minor elevation change for much of its course. Watch your footing in places, especially if the rocky surface is wet. Otherwise, marvel at the many views along the way as the blue-blazed path leads to numerous open ledges. The final stretch swings left into the shade of spruce trees and rapidly descends switchbacks to a junction.

Turn right onto the Valley Trail. A relaxing conclusion to the hike, this welcoming path drops gradually and crosses a dirt road in 0.4 mile (0.6 km). The final 0.3-mile (0.5-km) section begins easily before bending right and dropping swiftly to the parking area.

GOING FARTHER

From the summit, follow the eastern branch of the Beech Mountain Trail north to its trailhead. Hike across the parking area to explore the Beech Cliff Loop (see Hike 26) and then follow the Canada Cliffs Trail as it winds 0.8 mile (1.3 km) to the Valley Trail. Turn left and head south to Long Pond, completing a 4.1-mile (6.6-km) circuit.

WESTERN MOUNTAIN AND BASS HARBOR

Untouched by the infamous 1947 fire, Western Mountain's mostly forested slopes rise high above Long Pond, Bass Harbor Marsh, and Seal Cove Pond. To the south, classic coastal Maine scenery abounds from Bass Harbor, across Ship Harbor, to Seawall Beach. The more subtle natural beauty on this quieter side of Mount Desert Island can be enjoyed at a leisurely pace.

Most hikers in this region explore two well-used nature trails a short drive from Seawall Campground. Those looking to get away, even in the middle of the summer, head to Bernard and Mansell Mountains, where rugged forested trails lead to secluded viewpoints with pleasant ocean scenes that include Blue Hill Bay, Isle au Haut, and the Cranberry Isles.

This corner of the park has limited Island Explorer service but also less congestion. Be prepared to reach some trailheads on well-graded dirt roads that are closed during the winter season. Complement your day on the trails by snapping photos at Bass Harbor Head Lighthouse or enjoying a picnic at Seawall Beach.

OPPOSITE: *Ship Harbor Trail (Hike 31) visits many viewpoints overlooking the ocean.*

28 MANSELL MOUNTAIN AND LONG POND

Distance: 4.6-mile (7.4-km) loop
Elevation gain: 950 feet (290 m)
High point: 949 feet (289 m)
Difficulty: Challenging
Trail surface: Crushed stone, bog bridging, and uneven terrain
Map: Park brochure
GPS: 44.300225°N, 68.350068°W
Notes: Swimming prohibited; dogs not recommended

> A challenging hike in Mount Desert Island's less-frequented corner, this rewarding loop showcases amazing trail craftsmanship, rugged natural beauty, and forests ringing with the trills of Swainson's thrush and calls of magnolia warblers.

GETTING THERE

From the Somesville Fire Station, follow Route 102 south 4.8 miles (7.7 km) toward Southwest Harbor before turning right onto Seal Cove Road. Bear right on Long Pond Road in 0.6 mile (1 km) and then drive 1.2 miles (1.9 km) to the trailhead. Find parking near the pond's shore and additional spots just before.

ON THE TRAIL

The Long Pond Trail begins at the western side of the pond's pumping station, a small building near the parking lot. Follow this welcoming path past a junction with the Cold Brook Trail and along the pond's shoreline 0.2 mile (0.3 km) to the base of the Perpendicular Trail.

Turn left and immediately begin a steep ascent. Slithering up switchbacks, the path soon exits the forest into a large boulder field. Plod higher, aided by an elaborate rock staircase. Views of Long Pond's blue waters are impressive before you rise into the boreal forest. Wrap around granite ledges, including an especially impressive one near the trail's halfway point.

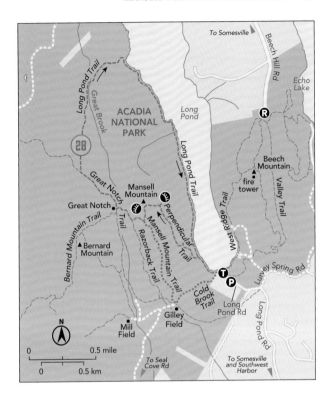

The path descends briefly before resuming the climb alongside a small stream. Rock steps and bridges lead up the valley to a large granite bluff, 0.7 mile (1.1 km) from Long Pond. Enjoy impressive views out to the Cranberry Isles, then check out the spur leading north les than 0.1 mile (0.2 km) to an outlook with views toward Sargent Mountain.

The Perpendicular Trail resumes its course through a forested wetland before scrambling up to Mansell Mountain's wooded summit in 0.2 mile (0.3 km). From the 949-foot (289-m) high point, follow the Mansell Mountain Trail south. It passes a sign for Lookout Point, where a short spur departs

A hiker takes a break at one of Long Pond's many shoreline vistas.

right to views of Blue Hill Bay. In 0.1 mile (0.2 km), arrive at a three-way intersection. Turn right toward Great Notch.

Watch your footing as the ledge-covered route descends roughly and rapidly 0.1 mile (0.2 km) into a dense spruce forest. A short incline leads to another three-way junction. Bear right onto the Razorback Trail, which soon traverses a narrow ledge that offers pleasant views of Blue Hill Bay. Surrounded by trees once again, drop 0.2 mile (0.3 km) into Great Notch. This narrow gap divides Western Mountain's two primary peaks—Mansell to the east and Bernard to the west.

From the 640-foot (195-m) high saddle, follow the Great Notch Trail north. It descends an earthen staircase and then proceeds easily 0.4 mile (0.6 km) to a junction with the Long Pond Trail. Turn right onto the wide corridor. It leads over inviting terrain and crosses Great Brook in 0.9 mile (1.4 km). Drop another 0.3 mile (0.5 km) to the edge of the scenic pond.

Swinging south, follow the cedar-lined shoreline 1.5 miles (2.4 km). Mostly flat, the route features numerous ledges that are ideal for picnics and photography—remember that swimming is prohibited. Before passing the base of the Perpendicular Trail, climb up a small incline only to drop back to the water's edge as quickly. Enjoy views of Beech Mountain's ledge-covered slopes and scan the waters for birds while concluding the circuit. With a little luck, you may see a spotted sandpiper bobbing its tail as it feeds along the shore.

OTHER OPTIONS

Combine the Long Pond, Perpendicular, Mansell Mountain, and Cold Brook Trails to complete a 2.4-mile (3.9-km) loop. The Mansell Mountain Trail showcases many vistas from its granite ledges before dropping to the Gilley Field parking area. Use the Cold Brook Trail to return to Long Pond.

29 WESTERN MOUNTAIN

Distance: 3.7-mile (6-km) loop
Elevation gain: 1250 feet (380 m)
High point: 1071 feet (326 m)
Difficulty: Challenging
Trail surface: Granite ledges, bog bridging, and uneven terrain
Map: Park brochure
GPS: 44.296674°N, 68.357133°W
Notes: Access road closed late fall through early spring

> Escape the crowds on Park Loop Road by exploring this hidden loop up Western Mountain's granite ridges and under its dense spruce canopy en route to hidden geological features, pleasant ocean vistas, and wildlife-rich, high-elevation habitats.

GETTING THERE

From the Somesville Fire Station, follow Route 102 south 4.8 miles (7.7 km) toward Southwest Harbor before turning right onto Seal Cove Road. Drive 1.4 miles (2.3 km) and enter the park as the pavement turns to dirt. Continue straight 0.7 mile

The Razorback Trail visits a series of open ledges.

(1.1 km) and bear right onto Heath Brook Road. In 0.4 mile (0.6 km), turn right on Western Mountain Road. Proceed 1.2 miles (1.9 km) to a three-way intersection. Turn right on Mill Field Road to reach the Gilley Field Trailhead in 0.2 mile (0.3 km).

ON THE TRAIL

Western Mountain, which is comprised of Mansell and Bernard Mountains, features deep valleys, rugged ridges, and less prominent knobs than those found in other parts of the park. This parking area and another at nearby Mill Field provide access to five trails, offering more than ten loop options. See Other Options to amend the described hike.

Begin on the Gilley Trail, a wide path that parallels the dirt road 0.1 mile (0.2 km) to a junction. Turn right on the 0.9-mile (1.4-km) Razorback Trail. It rises slowly at first, but the slope quickly steepens as the landscape of scattered rocks and thick evergreens transitions to granite ledges and open vistas.

Take your time and weave up the incline. Occasional rock scrambles lead to more expansive views of Frenchboro,

Swans Island, and Bernard Mountain. Reach a well-marked junction high on the ridge. Stay left on the Razorback Trail as it heads over rocky pinnacles showcasing scenes of Blue Hill Bay. The route swings west and descends 0.2 mile (0.3 km) to a four-way intersection in Great Notch, a 640-foot (195-m) high gap that separates Mansell and Bernard Mountains.

Heading southwest out of Great Notch, hike straight on the Bernard Mountain Trail. Over the next 0.5 mile (0.8 km), this rugged route winds around ledges, over roots, and eventually up to the 930-foot (283-m) summit of Knight Nubble. Just before reaching this wooded peak, check out the short spur that heads left to a scenic outlook of Mansell Mountain and Southwest Harbor. Dropping quickly from the high point, the main trail reaches an intersection at Little Notch.

Continue straight (southwest) and make your way up 0.1 mile (0.2 km) to a short outlook trail on the right that offers modest views. Ascend another 0.1 mile (0.2 km) to the top of Bernard Mountain. At 1071 feet (326 m), this is Western Mountain's highest point. There are only views of the surrounding vegetation, or with a little luck, resident wildlife such as red-breasted nuthatches creeping and foraging along the spruce limbs.

Remain on the Bernard Mountain Trail as it heads south and then west, descending gradually 0.5 mile (0.8 km) through a pleasant forested landscape. Swing sharply left at an intersection with the West Ledge Trail. Although the route begins to drop more aggressively and the terrain is a bit rocky, the footing is not too difficult to navigate. Slowly, more hardwood trees appear, and the incline eases. In 1 mile (1.6 km), reach a trailhead at a small cul-de-sac at Mill Field.

Follow the main road over a bridge and then immediately turn left. The dirt road leads uphill 0.1 mile (0.2 km). Upon reaching the small, dammed "reservoir" in the stream, turn right onto a short path that leads quickly to the Gilley Trail.

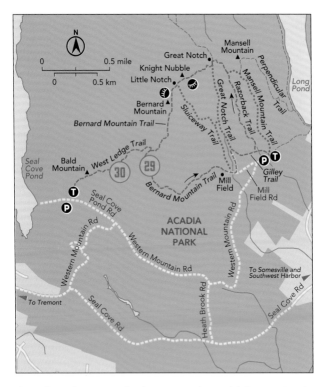

Complete the circuit by bearing right and hiking 0.3 mile (0.5 km) to the parking area.

OTHER OPTIONS

A variety of alternative routes are accessible from this trailhead and nearby Mill Field. The Mansell Mountain Trail is a good substitute for the Razorback Trail over similar terrain. On the southern slopes of Bernard Mountain explore the Sluiceway or Great Notch Trails. Both are densely forested routes that parallel small streams. Each is roughly 1 mile (1.6 km) from the road to the ridge. The Sluiceway is steeper, but the footing on both is good.

30 BERNARD MOUNTAIN AND WEST LEDGE

Distance: 3 miles (4.8 km)
Elevation gain: 1050 feet (320 m)
High point: 1071 feet (326 m)
Difficulty: Moderate to challenging
Trail surface: Granite ledges and uneven terrain
Map: Park brochure
GPS: 44.292117°N, 68.387047°W
Notes: Access road closed late fall through early spring

Choose this quiet route to the top of Western Mountain's highest point, where solitude and picnic spots accompany stunning scenery of Blue Hill Bay from barren granite ledges.

GETTING THERE

From the Somesville Fire Station, follow Route 102 south 4.8 miles (7.7 km) toward Southwest Harbor before turning right onto Seal Cove Road. Drive 1.4 miles (2.3 km) and enter the park as the pavement turns to dirt. Continue straight 0.7 mile (1.1 km) and bear right onto Heath Brook Road. In 0.4 mile (0.6 km), turn left on Western Mountain Road. Proceed 0.9 mile (1.4 km), then stay right on Seal Cove Pond Road and drive 0.4 mile (0.6 km) to a small parking area on the left, just beyond the trailhead.

ON THE TRAIL

From the road's north side, the West Ledge Trail winds gradually through the mixed forest. It quickly swings left, rises more aggressively up exposed ledges, and then levels off. Head over the mostly wooded summit of Bald Mountain in 0.3 mile (0.5 km) and scan the surrounding forest for avian life, including northern flickers. One of the park's larger and more vocal woodpeckers, flickers display bright yellow underneath their wings and a large white patch on their backsides.

Nearly half of the West Ledge Trail lives up to its name.

After a brief descent, climb steeply through the thinning forest canopy. As you emerge atop open sections of granite ledges, enjoy pleasant views west across islands, coves, and distant peninsulas. The panorama grows more expansive with increased elevation, with the best vista coming at approximately 0.6 mile (1 km) from the start. Grab a snack and take in the scenery of nearby Swans Island, more distant Isle au Haut, and the Camden Hills on the far side of Penobscot Bay. The remaining 0.3 mile (0.5 km) of the trail offers a few more ocean views, but the route traverses an increasingly forested landscape.

Reach a junction and stay left, joining the Bernard Mountain Trail. With minor elevation gain, the inviting path weaves easily 0.5 mile (0.8 km) through the boreal forest to the summit of Bernard Mountain. At 1071 feet (326 m) above sea level, Bernard is the highest peak on Mount Desert Island's western side. Since the high point is completely forested, continue 0.1 mile (0.2 km) farther to a spur that leads left to a bench and modest outlook. Complete the hike by retracing your steps 1.5 miles (2.4 km) back to the trailhead.

31 SHIP HARBOR TRAIL

Distance: 1.4-mile (2.3-km) loop
Elevation gain: 200 feet (60 m)
High point: 50 feet (15 m)
Difficulty: Easy
Trail surface: Crushed stone, bog bridging, and uneven terrain
Map: Park brochure
GPS: 44.231733°N, 68.325560°W
Notes: Privy at trailhead

> One of the park's most accessible hikes throughout the year, the Ship Harbor Trail offers incredible rewards for the effort, including rugged coastal beauty along with ample opportunities to enjoy intimate views of sea ducks, tide pools, and other marine life.

GETTING THERE

From the junction of Clark Point Road and Route 102 (Main Street) in Southwest Harbor, follow Route 102 south 2.3 miles (3.7 km) to Bass Harbor and then turn left onto Route 102A. Follow Route 102A 2.3 miles (3.7 km) to the trailhead and parking area on the right.

ON THE TRAIL

The well-manicured trail weaves down a grassy slope to a kiosk and quickly enters the maritime forest. In 0.1 mile

Surf pounding Ship Harbor's rocky entrance

(0.2 km), reach an intersection where the trail begins the first of two loops that form a figure eight. Stay left and follow the wide path as it meanders over the low, rolling terrain past spruce, fir, and an occasional white pine. The moist air sustains a thick carpet of moss, painting the ground in various shades of green. Reach a second intersection in 0.2 mile (0.3 km).

Continue left and begin the 0.6-mile (1-km) southern loop, which is slightly more challenging than the northern circuit. Rise to the top of a 50-foot (15-m) ridge. The trail proceeds through small openings between groves of trees. Meander over sections of bog bridging and occasional rocky terrain before descending to the peninsula's rugged point.

Near an information panel, follow an unmarked trail left to the shore. The many rocks and exposed ledges provide excellent spots to relax and enjoy classic coastal scenery, including crashing waves, sailboats, lobster buoys, and sea creatures thriving in nearby tide pools (see "Tide Pooling" sidebar). Watch your footing on the slippery rocks and remain alert to incoming surf.

TIDE POOLING

If you choose to explore tide pools, remember that intertidal creatures are fragile and easily injured. The park offers the following safety tips: do not wade or sit in tide pools; rocks and algae are slippery; watch your step; never turn your back on the ocean as rogue waves can occur at any time; wear suitable clothing and closed-toe shoes; sea creatures live everywhere, so be careful where you place your feet; if you move animals or rocks, return them to the same spot; do not pry animals from rocks as it may injure them in the process; re-cover animals you find under rocks or seaweed so they won't dry out; and remember that all living creatures are protected in the park so please take only pictures.

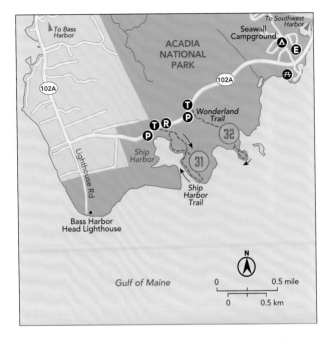

The return journey leads to the edge of Ship Harbor. In less than a quarter mile, you'll arrive at its mouth. From a rocky promontory, watch the water rush through the inlet's narrow opening as the tide rises in or flushes out as it ebbs. This is the trail's rockiest section, but the ruggedness does not last long. Be sure to check out the spur exiting left. It ends at a small spit in the heart of the harbor. Continuing on, you'll soon arrive at the end of the southern loop.

Swing left and continue to skirt the secluded cove. Buffleheads, goldeneyes, and other waterfowl are drawn to the harbor's deep, well-protected waters. Look for these sea ducks diving below the surface in search of food. The final stretch leads to a small outcrop high above the water, then bends right and heads down the slope to complete the circuit. Turn left to hike back to the trailhead.

32 WONDERLAND TRAIL

Distance: 1.4 miles (2.3 km)
Elevation gain: 80 feet (25 m)
High point: 55 feet (17 m)
Difficulty: Easy
Trail surface: Granite ledges and crushed stone
Map: Park brochure
GPS: 44.233811°N, 68.320009°W

> This short journey leads to an alluring location to watch the rising or setting sun and showcases attractive mountain views, picturesque coastal scenes, diverse bird habitats, and plentiful spots to enjoy cool ocean breezes on hot summer days.

GETTING THERE

From the junction of Clark Point Road and Route 102 (Main Street) in Southwest Harbor, follow Route 102 south 2.3 miles (3.7 km) to Bass Harbor and then turn left onto Route 102A. Follow Route 102A 2.7 miles (4.3 km) to the trailhead and parking area on the right.

ON THE TRAIL

From the parking lot's eastern edge, a narrow trail leads immediately to a much wider corridor. The Wonderland Trail used to be an old dirt road but today serves only as a welcoming footpath to the shore. Follow this route to the right, toward the alluring sound of waves and the raucous calls of gulls.

Winding past forested bogs and tunneling through walls of thick vegetation, the trail eventually ascends a low hill. Enjoy the forgiving terrain and stay alert for songbirds flitting in the nearby canopy. With some patience, you may encounter the diminutive black-throated green warbler. Despite its name, this prolific Acadia bird is more noteworthy for its bright yellow cheeks.

An inviting shoreline surrounds the Wonderland Trail's final stretch.

With each step, the peninsula narrows and soon you arrive at the hike's first ocean views, where unmarked spurs lead left and right to the water's edge. To the west, explore an inviting crescent-shaped beach and its many attractive picnic spots.

Follow the main route straight to a three-way junction, located 0.6 mile (1 km) from the start. Here, a 0.2-mile (0.3-km) loop winds easily around the tip of the peninsula. In a clockwise direction, the circuit heads left through the dark spruce canopy. Catch ocean scenery and glimpses of Acadia's highest summits rising to the northeast through the many gaps in the forest.

Upon arriving at the peninsula's southernmost tip, take advantage of the unmarked spurs leading left to the rocky shoreline. Use caution with incoming surf and explore the tide pools and exposed granite surfaces. Offshore, look for rafts of common eiders floating in the waves. The black-and-white drakes are more noticeable, but the brown hens with young are generally more common in the summer. These sea ducks feast on mussels and find protection in floating beds of rockweed.

Complete the loop and then retrace your steps 0.6 mile (1 km) to the start. This can be a crowded trail, so consider avoiding it in the middle of the day. Campers staying at nearby Seawall Campground should explore this trail first thing in the morning or late in the afternoon. It is also a less crowded option than nearby Bass Harbor Head Lighthouse for capturing the sunset.

ISLE AU HAUT

Acadia's most remote section is on the southern half of Isle au Haut, a more than 8000-acre (3200-hectare) island with a year-round population of around fifty residents that increases fivefold during the summer. From the island's 543-foot (166-m) high point located on private land, a forested ridge descends through the park, leading south to dramatic shoreline vantage points at Barred Harbor, Squeaker Cove, and Western Head.

Hiking Isle au Haut is far different from hiking Mount Desert Island. Be prepared for a slower-paced day on less manicured trails, where amenities and services are scarce. At the same time, enjoy paths where the sounds of waves, seabirds, and ocean breezes drown out the handful of other hikers present.

Reach Isle au Haut using the passenger-only Mail Boat service out of Stonington (see "Getting to Isle au Haut" sidebar). Limited camping is available at Duck Harbor for those who reserve well in advance, allowing for multiple days on the island. Otherwise spend a half day exploring the trails and enjoy a pleasant voyage on both ends of the journey.

OPPOSITE: *Isle au Haut's rugged Cliff Trail (Hike 33)*

33 WESTERN HEAD

Distance: **5.8-mile (9.3-km) loop**
Elevation gain: **600 feet (185 m)**
High point: **110 feet (34 m)**
Difficulty: **Moderate to challenging**
Trail surface: **Granite ledges, bog bridging, rock steps, and uneven terrain**
Map: **Park's Isle au Haut map**
GPS: **44.028592°N, 68.652883°W**
Notes: **Privy and fresh water available near trailhead**

> This loop hike around Western Head's rugged cliffs, secluded coves, and dramatic shoreline explores one of Acadia's wildest and most spectacular landscapes, yet few park visitors experience it.

GETTING THERE

From Stonington, take the Isle au Haut Mail Boat to the Duck Harbor Landing (see "Getting to Isle au Haut" sidebar).

GETTING TO ISLE AU HAUT

In Stonington, at the southern end of Deer Isle (accessed by bridge via Route 15), find the Isle au Haut Boat Services at the southern end of Seabreeze Avenue 0.1 mile (0.2 km) from Route 15; parking is limited. From May through October the Mail Boat makes two daily stops at Duck Harbor: late morning and midafternoon. This schedule serves campers and allows for roughly four hours of exploration for day visitors. If camping is not an option and you want to spend more hours on the island, early morning and late afternoon boat service provides access to the Isle au Haut Town Landing near a trailhead at the park's northern end. For the latest information, schedule, and rates, visit www.isleauhautferryservice.com.

The Goat Trail features numerous dramatic coastal viewpoints.

ON THE TRAIL

From the Duck Harbor Landing and Campground, take the path that leads east 0.1 mile (0.2 km) to Western Head Road (open only to emergency vehicles). Turn right onto the wide route. Lined with sweet fern, spruce, and balsam fir, it rises gradually past the start of the Duck Harbor Mountain Trail on the left and in 0.4 mile (0.6 km) reaches the Western Head Trail.

Turn right on the much narrower 1.3-mile (2.1-km) route. Swinging southwest, this undulating path leads to a small cobble beach before curving left. There are minor elevation changes, but the footing is occasionally rough. Parallel the scenic shoreline and take your time to explore the many beaches and headlands until you reach a junction with the Cliff Trail. Before heading north, explore the spur leading right to a secluded gravel beach near the Western Ear. While this small island is accessible during low tide, beware of rising water.

For 0.2 mile (0.3 km) the Cliff Trail weaves around ledges and through windswept forest, then soon reveals the island's most spectacular ocean vistas. Remain near the rugged shoreline over the next 0.5 mile (0.8 km). You will have countless

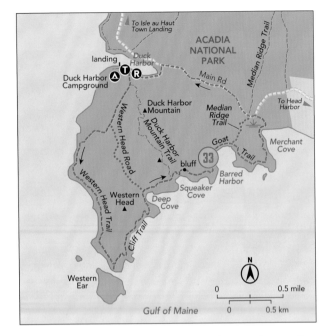

views of waves crashing into granite ledges and water funneling through narrow chasms. Watch your step, especially on the rocky sections closest to the shore and the occasional scramble to scenic promontories perched high above the surf.

The trail ends at the southern terminus of Western Head Road. Follow this corridor 0.1 mile (0.2 km) to reach the Goat Trail. Turn right and parallel Deep Cove's shoreline before heading through a dense boreal forest to the eastern end of the Duck Harbor Mountain Trail in 0.3 mile (0.5 km). To the right lies Squeaker Cove, a cobble beach that generates soothing sounds as it welcomes incoming waves.

Continue along the Goat Trail as it tunnels through walls of spruce that often welcome flocks of white-winged crossbills. Very vocal, these red (sometimes ranging into yellow and orange) birds are uniquely adapted to feed on cones.

Rise to a scenic bluff with extensive southern views before descending once again.

The path moderates en route to Barred Harbor and a junction with the Median Ridge Trail. Located 0.9 mile (1.4 km) from Squeaker Cove, this secluded harbor offers protection for boats, but rocks prevent ingress and egress during low tide.

Complete the Goat Trail's final 0.8-mile (1.4-km) stretch by remaining close to the shore. This lightly used section winds up and over a low ridge before arriving at Merchant Cove. Follow the bog bridging across an extensive wetland and then rise quickly to a dirt road.

Turn left and follow Main Road west. It immediately crosses the Median Ridge Trail then heads up and over a small incline. In 0.8 mile (1.3 km), turn left onto Western Head Road and hike 0.4 mile (0.6 km) back to the Duck Harbor Landing.

OTHER OPTIONS

Consider two possible shortcuts. After completing the Cliff Trail, follow Western Head Road 1.5 miles (2.4 km) back to Duck Harbor to complete a 4-mile (6.4-km) loop. From Barred Harbor, use the Median Ridge Trail to reach the dirt road and shorten the hike by 0.5 mile (0.8 km). Keep both options in mind, especially to avoid missing the ferry back to Stonington.

34 EBENS HEAD

Distance: 2.7 miles (4.3 km)
Elevation gain: 150 feet (45 m)
High point: 40 feet (12 m)
Difficulty: Easy
Trail surface: Granite ledges, bog bridging, crushed stone, and uneven terrain
Map: Park's Isle au Haut map

The Ebens Head Trail hugs the rocky shoreline.

GPS: 44.028592°N, 68.652883°W
Notes: Privy and fresh water available near trailhead

> Enjoy an attractive afternoon picnic spot before catching the ferry back to Stonington. This short hike to cobble beaches, rocky shores, and a promontory with serene coastal views is also a pleasant early morning jaunt after spending the night at the Duck Harbor Campground.

GETTING THERE

From Stonington, take the Isle au Haut Mail Boat to the Duck Harbor Landing (see "Getting to Isle au Haut" sidebar in Hike 33).

ON THE TRAIL

From the Duck Harbor Landing, take the path that leads east 0.1 mile (0.2 km) to Western Head Road (open only to emergency vehicles). Follow the dirt road left. It wraps around the inner harbor, which during low tide welcomes foraging gulls and shorebirds. Cross an inlet stream and rise to an intersection with Main Road.

It's difficult to imagine today, but this secluded corner of the park has a long history of human activity. For centuries, the Wabanaki and early European settlers were lured here for its plentiful waterfowl. In the nineteenth century the narrow waterbody was lined with homes, wharves, docks, and a bustling fishing community.

Follow Main Road left (although cars are infrequent, they are allowed here) and parallel the harbor's northern shore. With little elevation change, walk 0.4 mile (0.6 km) to where the Duck Harbor Trail departs right. Stay on the road less than 0.1 mile (0.2 km) to reach the Ebens Head Trail.

Departing left, the narrower path enters the boreal forest. Weave along the shoreline and enjoy an occasional glimpse of the salt water upon reaching a short spur in 0.2 mile

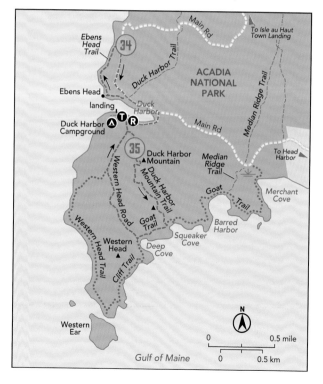

(0.3 km). Bear left and scramble to the top of Ebens Head, a small, grassy pinnacle that rises steeply above the surf.

Some believe the head was named after a local nineteenth century fisherman, while others think it honors one of Duck Harbor's earliest settlers. Either way, today it offers alluring ocean views west toward the Fox Islands. Ebens Head is also a good place to spot porpoises feeding in the swirling surf. And look for common guillemots, a black-and-white seabird that displays its distinctive orange feet when diving for food.

Rejoin the main trail as it hugs the shore to the north. It crosses granite ledges and dissects spruce forest, with modest ups and downs. Reach a large gravel beach in 0.5 mile (0.8 km). At the northern end of the expanse, where a sign points to the road, head back into the mossy woods. The trail quickly ends. Turn right, hike 0.4 mile (0.6 km) along Main Road to complete the loop, and then retrace your steps 0.8 mile (1.3 km) to the Duck Harbor Landing.

35 DUCK HARBOR MOUNTAIN

Distance: 3-mile (4.8-km) loop
Elevation gain: 500 feet (150 m)
High point: 308 feet (94 m)
Difficulty: Challenging
Trail surface: Crushed stone, granite ledges, bog bridging, and uneven terrain
Map: Park's Isle au Haut map
GPS: 44.028592°N, 68.652883°W
Notes: Privy and fresh water available near trailhead

Isle au Haut's most challenging hike, this aggressive scramble up and over Duck Harbor Mountain's open granite ledges features extensive views of classic Maine coast scenery.

Views of Duck Harbor from the mountain that bears its name

GETTING THERE

From Stonington, take the Isle au Haut Mail Boat to the Duck Harbor Landing (see "Getting to Isle au Haut" sidebar in Hike 33).

ON THE TRAIL

From the Duck Harbor Landing, take the path that leads east 0.1 mile (0.2 km) to Western Head Road (open only to emergency vehicles). Veer right onto the wider footpath as it gradually ascends 0.1 mile (0.2 km) to the start of the Duck Harbor Mountain Trail on the left.

Begin the challenging 0.4-mile (0.6-km) trek, which wastes little time scrambling up the granite hillside to the mountain's high point. The rugged trail climbs very steeply and quickly emerges onto the first of many open ledges. On the western horizon enjoy scenes of the Camden Hills rising over the Fox Islands. Weaving past blueberry bushes, sheep laurel, and stunted spruce, the path drops briefly into thicker woods before one final climb leads to the 308-foot (94-m) summit.

Catch your breath and enjoy the surrounding beauty. Although it is mostly downhill from here, the 0.7-mile (1.1-km) route to Squeaker Cove is far from straightforward.

Head from the summit in a southerly direction and while descending listen for the high-pitched call of cedar waxwings. These sleek birds are adept at catching insects in flight and add flashes of red and yellow to the otherwise green surroundings.

The trail briefly levels off and heads over an open ledge before losing more elevation. Wind through a pleasant boreal forest before beginning the trail's final stretch. Scramble up and over a series of steep, rocky knolls. The path does not let up much until it concludes at a junction with the Goat Trail. In spots, you may need to use your hands to pull yourself up or get on all fours to drop down. Use caution, especially if the terrain is wet, and marvel at the spectacular views of the approaching shoreline.

At Squeaker Cove, steps lead to the cobble beach. This is a great place to hang out, enjoy the island's quiet serenity, and scan just above the rolling waves for common terns zigzagging in search of small fish.

Resume the loop by heading southwest along the Goat Trail. Hike through a dense spruce forest en route to Deep Cove. In 0.3 mile (0.5 km) reach a junction with Western Head Road. To complete your adventure, turn right onto the old road for a relaxing conclusion. After a modest elevation gain, pass a junction with the Western Head Trail in 0.9 mile (1.4 km). A moderate, steady descent leads to the campground and Duck Harbor Landing 0.5 mile (0.8 km) farther.

GOING FARTHER

Lengthen this hike by combining it with adjacent trails (see Hike 33). Rather than heading back when you first encounter Western Head Road, extend the loop to include the Cliff and Western Head Trails. Or, upon reaching Squeaker Cove, hike east and north along the Goat Trail to Merchant Cove before taking Main Road to Duck Harbor. Both options result in a 4.2-mile (6.8-km) circuit.

36 BOWDITCH MOUNTAIN

Distance: 8.1-mile (13-km) loop
Elevation gain: 1050 feet (320 m)
High point: 470 feet (143 m)
Difficulty: Challenging
Trail surface: Granite ledges, bog bridging, crushed stone, and uneven terrain
Map: Park's Isle au Haut map
GPS: 44.028592°N, 68.652883°W
Notes: Privy and fresh water available near trailhead

> While lacking in spectacular scenery, this hike through the heart of Isle au Haut lures those seeking remoteness, quiet natural beauty, and inviting forests where wild creatures greatly outnumber those walking on two feet.

GETTING THERE

From Stonington, take the Isle au Haut Mail Boat to the Duck Harbor Landing (see "Getting to Isle au Haut" sidebar in Hike 33).

ON THE TRAIL

The described hike is a good option for those camping over-night at Duck Harbor. If you are spending only one day on the island, see Other Options for ways to amend the hike.

From the Duck Harbor Landing, take the path that leads east 0.1 mile (0.2 km) to Western Head Road (open only to emergency vehicles). Turn left on the wide dirt road. Continue around the harbor, cross an inlet stream, and rise to an intersection.

Follow Main Road's dirt surface to the left (cars are allowed here) and hike 0.4 mile (0.6 km) to the start of the Duck Harbor Trail on the right. Heading north away from the water, this forested route rises quickly up rocky terrain. Level off, descend gently, and cross Main Road in 0.8 mile (1.3 km).

The trail drops another 0.2 mile (0.3 km) to a junction with the Deep Cove Trail, a pleasant 0.1-mile (0.2-km) diversion to the shoreline.

Over the next 1.1 miles (1.8 km), the Duck Harbor Trail heads north with little elevation change, but the footing is occasionally rough. After a brief forested stretch, it closely hugs the shoreline of Moores Harbor, providing many intimate, photo-worthy water views. Follow the blue blazes carefully, especially along the beaches, and then rise easily to another junction with Main Road. Pick up the trail on the other side and immediately reach the Bowditch Trail on the right.

Named after Ernest Bowditch, whose heirs donated his Isle au Haut properties to the park in 1943, this lightly used path follows a small stream while heading deep into the island's interior. Winding through lush wetlands, it features bog bridging, but in many places a thick carpet of moss, ferns, and plants obscures the footing. The tread can be slippery, biting insects may be plentiful, and your feet could get wet, especially following rain events. On the positive side, wild orchids, songbirds, pitcher plants, and other bog-friendly flora and fauna abound.

Climbing out of the wetlands, the footing quickly becomes drier. Level off and briefly enter private property near the trail's halfway point. The route turns sharply right, reenters Acadia, and winds south along the rolling ridge. After passing over the wooded summit areas of Jerusalem and Bowditch Mountains, the 2-mile (3.2-km) trail ends at a three-way junction.

Now in the heart of a sparsely populated, offshore island, you are far away from the sights and sounds of human activity. Although forested today, in the mid-eighteenth century much of the surrounding landscape was pastureland grazed by more than a thousand sheep. Turn right and follow the Long Pond Trail as it descends through the inviting hardwood forest that has reclaimed the land.

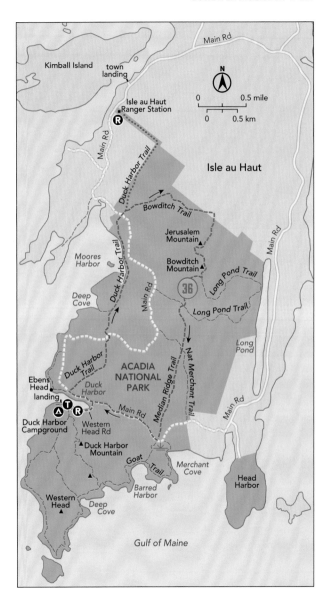

Mosses thrive on the lightly used Bowditch Trail.

In 0.5 mile (0.8 km), stay straight and join the Median Ridge Trail. It quickly regains some of the recent elevation loss only to drop once again to a four-way junction with the Nat Merchant Trail in 0.5 mile (0.8 km). Remain on the Median Ridge Trail as it weaves 1 mile (1.6 km) past forested wetlands, alongside a ledge-covered slope, and then down to Main Road.

Follow the dirt road right to return to Duck Harbor. It leads easily 0.8 mile (1.3 km) to Western Head Road. Turn left at the junction and hike 0.4 mile (0.6 km) east to the Duck Harbor Landing.

OTHER OPTIONS

Take the first ferry to Isle au Haut and get off at the town landing early in the morning. Follow the pavement 0.5 mile (0.8 km) south to the park's ranger station and access the northern end of the Duck Harbor Trail. Hike 1.3 miles (2.1 km) from the ranger station to reach the Bowditch Trail junction. Remain on the Duck Harbor Trail or turn left onto the Bowditch Trail to make your way to the island's southern trails. Explore Western Head (see Hikes 33 and 35) before grabbing the midafternoon ferry from Duck Harbor to Stonington.

SCHOODIC PENINSULA

Forming the eastern shore of Frenchman Bay, Schoodic Peninsula is known for its granite ledges, cobble beaches, and secluded coves. Photographers and artists are drawn to its southernmost point where the ocean pounds the granite and the sun's rays sparkle on the surf. Through the heart of the peninsula, the land rises to the mostly wooded summits of Schoodic Head and Buck Cove Mountain.

Schoodic's trails offer generous rewards in exchange for modest effort. North of the park, hikers can explore more challenging terrain by scaling Schoodic Mountain or surrounding peaks within Maine's Donnell Pond Public Land. Both the state and federal lands are ideal destinations to escape summer crowds and enjoy a more relaxed Maine coast adventure.

The loop road around the peninsula offers easy access to the park's trailheads, and Island Explorer buses provide a convenient alternative service, especially for those camping at Schoodic Woods. A great way to cap off a day of hiking is to hop on a bike to tour Schoodic's network of bike paths.

OPPOSITE: *Lower Harbor's protected waters often attract birds and other wildlife (Hike 37).*

37 LOWER HARBOR

Distance: 2.1-mile (3.4-km) loop
Elevation gain: 200 feet (60 m)
High point: 150 feet (46 m)
Difficulty: Easy to moderate
Trail surface: Crushed stone, bog bridging, and uneven terrain
Map: Park's Schoodic map
GPS: 44.380134°N, 68.066559°W
Notes: Restroom at trailhead

A good introduction to the Schoodic Peninsula, this short hike takes advantage of friendly topography to get you easily to the welcoming inner reaches of Winter Harbor, where the undulating flight of belted kingfishers accents the serene views.

GETTING THERE

From the center of Winter Harbor, follow Route 186 east toward Birch Harbor. Drive 0.5 mile (0.8 km) and turn right onto Schoodic Loop Road. Head south 0.9 mile (1.4 km), then turn left toward the Schoodic Woods Ranger Station and Campground. In 0.1 mile (0.2 km), turn right into the day-use parking area.

ON THE TRAIL

Follow the signs to the ranger station, added to the park in 2015 with the adjacent campground. These new amenities are part of a more than 1400-acre (565-hectare) anonymous donation to Acadia that included funds to support the construction of buildings, campsites, and recreational paths, including this trail to Lower Harbor.

Pick up the bike path behind the ranger station and follow the multiuse corridor to the left toward Winter Harbor. It quickly crosses the campground entrance road before

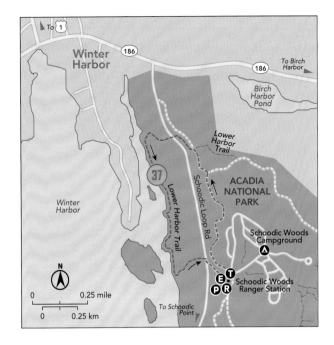

continuing over mostly level terrain. Look for wildlife signs, including scat left by coyotes and other resident mammals. In 0.6 mile (1 km), head left at a junction of bike paths. Continue another 0.2 mile (0.3 km) to reach the Lower Harbor Trail.

Bear left onto the much narrower hiking trail. Across bog bridging and through the forest, the route winds 0.1 mile (0.2 km) to the edge of Schoodic Loop Road. Use caution crossing (there is two-way traffic) and resume your journey. The trail drops easily but quickly through the evergreen forest. Approach the shoreline quietly to increase the likelihood that shorebirds and waterfowl will be in sight when you arrive in 0.2 mile (0.3 km).

Swinging left, the path begins its most scenic portion. Remaining close to the water's edge throughout, it meanders

Enjoying a quiet spot on the Lower Harbor Trail (photo by Maria Fuentes)

south 0.7 mile (1.1 km). There are modest ups and downs, and the footing is a little rough in places. Take your time and watch your step. Otherwise, enjoy the many picturesque views of the water and offshore islands. Some vistas are from more distant perspectives, while others are along the shore itself.

Near a cluster of cedar trees, the trail turns abruptly left. Switchbacks lead up the slight incline. In 0.2 mile (0.3 km), reach Schoodic Loop Road one last time. Cross the pavement and follow the road to the ranger station. There is plenty of room on the shoulder, but be alert for traffic.

38 SCHOODIC HEAD AND BUCK COVE MOUNTAIN

Distance: 3.7 miles (6 km)
Elevation gain: 750 feet (230 m)
High point: 442 feet (134 m)
Difficulty: Moderate to challenging
Trail surface: Granite ledges, bog bridging, rock steps, and uneven terrain
Map: Park's Schoodic map
GPS: 44.380134°N, 68.066559°W
Notes: Requires Island Explorer; restroom at ranger station

> From Schoodic's highest point, this lightly traveled route ambles across the center of the peninsula, offering pleasant scenes of Downeast Maine, blueberry-draped ledges, and regenerating pine forests hiding remnants of the most recent ice age.

GETTING THERE

From the center of Winter Harbor, follow Route 186 east toward Birch Harbor. Drive 0.5 mile (0.8 km) and turn right onto Schoodic Loop Road. Head south 0.9 mile (1.4 km), then turn left toward the Schoodic Woods Ranger Station and Campground. In 0.1 mile (0.2 km), turn right into the day-use parking area.

ON THE TRAIL

At the ranger station, wait for the next Island Explorer (see Other Options for a suggested alternative route that does not require bus transportation). When you board the bus, inform the driver that you would like to stop at the East Trail. Enjoy a pleasant ride down to Schoodic Point and then north along the peninsula's eastern shore to reach the trailhead.

The East Trail is a short, steep climb that offers little opportunity to warm up. Fortunately, there are plenty of intriguing scenes along the way. Proceed slowly up the incline as granite ledges offer views east across the rocky coastline. In the woods, the path winds methodically, finding the route of least resistance. The moss-lined trail soon gives way to a thinning forest and exposed rock. Look for snowshoe hares feeding in the understory as you reach a junction 0.4 mile (0.6 km) from the start.

Turn right and hike 0.1 mile (0.2 km) to the 442-foot (134-m) summit of Schoodic Head. The highest point on the peninsula, this prominent pinnacle features an overlook with attractive views toward Petit Manan Island and its tall lighthouse. The island is a seabird nesting site for terns, razorbills, and Atlantic puffins managed by the Maine Coastal Islands National Wildlife Refuge.

Continue the journey north, joining the Buck Cove Mountain Trail. This less-frequented path descends steadily at first while winding through a thick spruce forest. The trail eases a bit and then heads across semi-open ledges that offer pleasant views. Another drop is followed by a brief ascent to the top of Buck Cove Mountain. This diminutive 228-foot (63-m) peak lies 0.9 mile (1.4 km) north of Schoodic Head, which can be seen to the south over the treetops.

Drop north into a forested wetland. Bog bridging eases the way as the trail arrives at the Wonsqueak Bike Path in 0.3 mile (0.5 km). To the left, you can reach the campground and ranger station in 1.3 miles (2.1 km). However, the more scenic and fun journey lies straight ahead.

Remain on the Buck Cove Mountain Trail. Over the next 0.8 mile (1.3 km), it scales mostly open terrain with views east toward a landscape of bays, islands, and distant peninsulas. Briefly coincide left with a bike path and then turn left back onto the narrower tread. Quickly arrive at another bike path. Take your time at the various intersections; all are well signed.

Head straight across the bike path to rejoin the hiking trail. Winding through an older stand of trees, the trail swings south of a large bog where you may find pitcher plants. It then arrives at the base of an extensive ledge. Remain below the base of the long slab and make your way through the dark boreal forest. The path eventually bends right and rises gently to another bike path crossing 0.7 mile (1.1 km) from the last.

After crossing the bike path, a brief 0.1 mile (0.2 km) jaunt through the woods leads to the day's final bike path crossing. This is followed by a steady but straightforward 0.2 mile (0.3 km) descent to the trailhead. The ranger station and parking area are located 0.3 mile (0.5 km) west. Walk along the pavement through the campground to complete the journey.

OTHER OPTIONS

If the Island Explorer is not an option, begin and end the hike from the Schoodic Woods Ranger Station. Follow the Buck Cove Mountain Trail 3.2 miles (5.1 km) to the summit of Schoodic Head. Retrace your steps 1.2 miles (1.9 km) and follow the Wonsqueak Bike Path 1.3 miles (2.1 km) to complete a 5.7-mile (9.2-km) trek. You will likely have little company along the way.

Schoodic Head features pleasant views to the east.

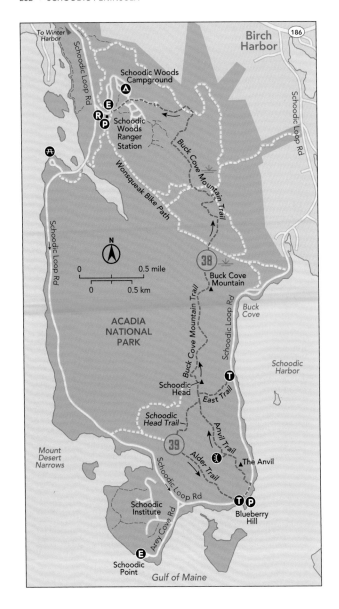

39 SCHOODIC HEAD AND THE ANVIL

Distance: 2.5-mile (4-km) loop
Elevation gain: 550 feet (170 m)
High point: 442 feet (134 m)
Difficulty: Moderate to challenging
Trail surface: Granite ledges, bog bridging, rock steps, and uneven terrain
Map: Park's Schoodic map
GPS: 44.338862°N, 68.046263°W

> The most alluring hike on the Schoodic Peninsula, this short loop near the point's southern tip combines rugged terrain and breathtaking vistas from above with a relaxing jaunt and diverse wildlife habitat below.

GETTING THERE

From the center of Winter Harbor, follow Route 186 east toward Birch Harbor. Drive 0.5 mile (0.8 km) and turn right onto Schoodic Loop Road. Follow Schoodic Loop Road 4.5 miles (7.2 km) and stay left. Continue 0.6 mile (1 km) to the Blueberry Hill parking area on the right.

ON THE TRAIL

Cross Schoodic Loop Road and follow it right for a few minutes to the start of the Anvil Trail on the left. This rocky path rises quickly up the rugged landscape. Winding around and over ledges, it reaches The Anvil's 190-foot (58-m) summit in 0.3 mile (0.5 km). The rough trail continues north over the rolling terrain and quickly reaches a spur left, leading to an overlook with attractive scenes west to Mount Desert Island.

The footing eases a bit as the trail crosses some open granite ledges, and reenters the evergreen forest. Rise steadily to the base of a large ledge. A steep climb leads higher up the slope. Hike across the root- and needle-covered tread to a

Cadillac Mountain dominates the western horizon from the Anvil Trail outlook.

more open expanse with limited views. The Anvil Trail ends at a three-way junction 0.9 mile (1.4 km) from the start.

Follow the Schoodic Head Trail right. With paths leaving left and right along the way, it winds easily 0.2 mile (0.3 km) across the top of the ridgeline to Schoodic Head, the peninsula's 442-foot (134-m) high point. Enjoy the overlook that boasts classic scenes of coastal Maine: bays, islands, and peninsulas to the east as far as the eyes can see.

Retrace your steps to the upper end of the Anvil Trail and turn right. Follow the Schoodic Head Trail southwest along semi-open granite ledges where you will catch impressive views west across the Mount Desert Narrows to Champlain and Cadillac Mountains. Snap a few shots—these are the final views of the day—and then resume the 0.5-mile (0.8-km) descent.

The upper sections of the trail are steep. Take your time, especially if the ground is wet. Bog bridging and rock steps are available to help navigate the way. Weaving around ledges and through narrow gaps in the rock, the route drops rapidly. As the trees grow taller and the incline becomes less intense, you will reach the trail's end.

Turn left onto the dirt road. It climbs easily 0.1 mile (0.2 km) to the start of the 0.6-mile (1-km) Alder Trail. Continue straight on this wide, forgiving footpath. With modest elevation changes, it passes a variety of plants. This diversity of habitats attracts many species of birds, particularly during migration. Listen for the calls of song sparrows and common yellowthroats ringing from the thick surrounding shrubbery, as northern parulas warble from the tree limbs above.

The trail becomes grassy before ending at the road. Safely cross the pavement. Before leaving, explore the rocky beach adjacent to the parking area. The tide will dictate how much exploring is possible.

DONNELL POND PUBLIC LAND

Comprising more than 14,000 acres (5600 hectares), this state-owned public land easily accessible off Route 1 between Ellsworth and the Schoodic Peninsula encompasses mountains, lakes, and natural features reminiscent of those in Acadia. Its peaks are visible from many Mount Desert Island summits. And for those looking to get off the beaten path and view Acadia National Park and Frenchman Bay from a different angle, Donnell Pond offers miles of quiet hiking trails to scenic vistas.

40 SCHOODIC MOUNTAIN

Distance: 2.8-mile (4.5-km) loop
Elevation gain: 1000 feet (300 m)
High point: 1069 feet (326 m)
Difficulty: Challenging
Trail surface: Granite ledges, bog bridging, and uneven terrain
Map: Maine Bureau of Parks and Lands map
GPS: 44.573966°N, 68.130138°W
Notes: Privy at trailhead and at Donnell Pond

Rather than viewing Schoodic Mountain's rocky summit from the Bar Harbor waterfront or from atop countless Mount Desert Island summits, choose this quiet half-day adventure on nearby state-owned public land for breathtaking views of Acadia's highest peaks and the area's stunning coastline.

GETTING THERE

From Route 1 in East Sullivan, follow Route 183 north 4.3 miles (6.9 km). At a sign for Donnell Pond Public Land, turn left onto the dirt surface of Schoodic Beach Road. Following signs pointing toward Schoodic Mountain, stay on this road 2.2 miles (3.5 km) until it ends at a large parking area.

ON THE TRAIL

The blue-blazed trail departs the western corner of the parking area, near a privy. Meander southwest through the thickly forested landscape and across a small brook. Slowly begin a steadier climb and rise between a lichen-covered ledge and a large boulder. As the trail swings right, the terrain levels briefly before ascending the rocky hillside. Past an outcrop with views of Black Mountain, rise through the thinning forest canopy onto semi-open ledges. Above, catch the first glimpse of the summit area through the numerous beech

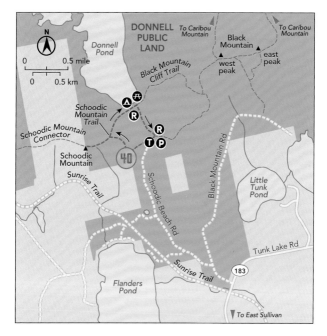

trees and arrive at a three-way intersection 0.9 mile (1.5 km) from the start.

Turn left for the 0.4-mile (0.6-km) final push to the top. Winding up and around steeper terrain, the path strikes a pleasant course past ocean and lake viewpoints. Each step brings you higher with fewer trees, until a last effort leads atop the barren summit area. Save for the communications tower, there is nothing to block the 360-degree views that include the highest summits of Acadia National Park, the Schoodic Peninsula, and sprawling Frenchman Bay. Watch your step and do your best to avoid trampling the fragile summit vegetation.

Return to the three-way intersection and head left toward the welcoming shore of Donnell Pond. At first gradual, the

Approaching Schoodic Mountain's open summit

intensity of the descent soon picks up; it is rocky in places, so take your time. The 0.6-mile (1-km) trail eventually reaches an old woods road where black-throated blue and blackburnian warblers provide a welcoming chorus of calls. The final dash leads easily toward the shore. Turn left, cross a small bridge, and make your way to the pond's sandy beach. A great place for picnics, backcountry camping, or a summer swim, Donnell Pond is anchored by towering peaks on both sides.

At the eastern end of the beach, a 0.5-mile (0.8-km) path completes the circuit. Follow an old road across a small bridge. Stay right at an intersection where the Black Mountain Cliff Trail leads left over another bridge. The route back to the trailhead is straightforward and climbs gently throughout.

OTHER OPTIONS

Consider a similar but slightly longer circuit leading to Black Mountain's barren east peak, where more adventurous hikers can significantly extend the excursion by venturing north on a loop over Caribou Mountain.

ACKNOWLEDGMENTS

I would be remiss if I failed to acknowledge the many people who played a part in the writing of this book. Special thanks to Acadia National Park employees Christie Anastasia, Alison Richardson, and Chris Wiebusch. All three took time out of their busy work schedules to provide advice and review draft materials. Thanks also to the Senator and Bonnie for providing a chateau and breakfast away from home. It is always fun to hear some lesser-known Mount Desert Island history.

Finally, extra-special thanks are due to my wife, Maria, daughter, Sabrina, and son, Anthony. You each provided needed support to make this book a reality. Thanks for your patience when I was away, both physically and mentally. I hope you remember most of our many adventures together. I know I will never forget enduring our all-day excursion to Western Head (how long did I say the hike was going to be?), spotting the coyote lurking on the slopes of Day Mountain, completing back-to-back-to-back circuits over Western and Beech Mountains, watching the sun set over Penobscot Bay and then the full moon rise over Eggemoggin Reach, scrambling up Cadillac and Dorr Mountains as the fall foliage approached its peak, and strolling around peaceful Hadlock Ponds.

OPPOSITE: *A quiet segment of the Penobscot Mountain Trail (Hike 18)*

CONTACT INFORMATION

VISITOR CENTERS

Acadia Gateway Center

In an effort to relieve traffic congestion, Acadia National Park is working with state and local partners to develop this new visitor center in Trenton. Conveniently located just off Route 3, minutes north of Mount Desert Island, the new facility will include parking, a small store, an information desk where visitors can purchase park passes, and a hub where visitors can hop on Island Explorer buses to access the park. It may be completed as early as 2022.

Gateway Center Drive
Trenton, ME 04605

Bar Harbor Chamber of Commerce

During winter and spring months, the Bar Harbor Chamber of Commerce shares its downtown location with the National Park Service, where visitors can talk with a park ranger and learn about Acadia National Park. Chamber staff provide information on lodging, restaurants, and local services.

2 Cottage Street
Bar Harbor, ME 04609
Open: December 1 through April 30

OPPOSITE: *Views of Jordan Pond from the North Bubble (Hike 13)*

Hulls Cove Visitor Center

Here you can find park passes and park rangers to answer your questions. Large, self-service maps and digital information screens help you plan your visit. There is a large parking area and access to Island Explorer buses. You can also purchase items from the America's National Parks Store located there.

25 Visitor Center Road
Bar Harbor, ME 04609
Open: May 1 through November 30

Schoodic Woods Ranger Station

Here you can find information, access Island Explorer buses, and purchase park passes.
54 Farview Drive
Winter Harbor, ME 04693
Open: Wednesday before Memorial Day until Columbus Day

Sieur de Monts Nature Center

Find exhibits, gather park information, and tour the Wild Gardens of Acadia. The parking lot is frequented by Island Explorer buses throughout the day in season.
47 Sweet Water Circle
Bar Harbor, ME 04609
Open: Early May through mid-October

Village Green Information Center

Here you can find information, access Island Explorer buses, and purchase park passes. Nearby street parking is limited, but the center is within walking distance of many hotels and inns.
19 Firefly Lane
Bar Harbor, ME 04609
Open: During peak season

CAMPGROUNDS

Acadia campgrounds are popular, hence finding a campsite upon arrival is a rare occurrence. Make your reservation in advance at www.recreation.gov. Advanced reservations are required for Duck Harbor, which fills up quickly once reservations are made available.

Blackwoods Campground

Location: 5.6 miles (9 km) south of the Bar Harbor Village Green on Route 3

Reservations: Sites are reservable up to six months in advance

Number of sites: 281

Open: Early May to mid-October

Other: Island Explorer bus service

Duck Harbor Campground

Location: Duck Harbor Landing, Isle au Haut

Reservations: Open on April 1

Number of sites: 5

Open: Mid-May through mid-October

Schoodic Woods Campground

Location: 1.5 miles (2.4 km) southeast of Winter Harbor on the Schoodic Peninsula

Reservations: Sites are reservable up to six months in advance

Number of sites: 89

Open: Mid-May through mid-October

Seawall Campground

Location: 4 miles (6.4 km) south of Southwest Harbor on Route 102A

Reservations: Sites are reservable up to six months in advance

Number of sites: 201

Open: Mid-May through mid-October

TRANSPORTATION

Island Explorer

www.exploreacadia.com

The Island Explorer features numerous bus routes linking hotels, inns, and campgrounds with destinations in Acadia National Park and neighboring village centers. These propane-powered vehicles offer Mount Desert Island and Schoodic Peninsula visitors free transportation to hiking trails, carriage roads, island beaches, and in-town shops and restaurants. Major hubs include the Bar Harbor Village Green and the Hulls Cove Visitor Center. The bus service operates from late June through mid-October.

Isle au Haut Boat Services

www.isleauhautferryservice.com

Isle au Haut Boat Services provides year-round scheduled passenger, freight, and mail service between Stonington and the Isle au Haut Town Landing and seasonal service to Duck Harbor.

OTHER

Abbe Museum

www.abbemuseum.org

The Abbe Museum inspires new learning about the Wabanaki Nations with every visit. In recent years, the Abbe has grown from a small trailside museum, privately operated within Acadia National Park, to an exciting contemporary museum in the heart of downtown Bar Harbor. In 2013, the museum became the first and only Smithsonian Affiliate in the state of Maine.

Friends of Acadia

https://friendsofacadia.org

A membership organization, Friends of Acadia (FOA) works with the park to identify places and projects where FOA's effective mix of private philanthropy, volunteerism, innovative leadership, and strong partnerships will most benefit the park's critical needs.

Jordan Pond House

https://jordanpondhouse.com

Jordan Pond House is home to a restaurant that has welcomed guests since 1893 to enjoy great views, its famous popovers, and tea from atop a hill overlooking Jordan Pond.

Land & Garden Preserve

www.gardenpreserve.org

This membership organization endeavors to "share the beauty of historic lands and gardens on Mount Desert Island," including on more than 1400 acres (567 hectares) of forestland abutting the park near Northeast Harbor.

Maine Coast Heritage Trust

www.mcht.org

A membership organization, Maine Coast Heritage Trust (MCHT) conserves and stewards Maine's coastal lands and islands for their renowned scenic beauty, ecological value, outdoor recreational opportunities, and contribution to community well-being. MCHT provides statewide conservation leadership through its work with land trusts, coastal communities, and partners like Acadia National Park.

INDEX

OPPOSITE: *Moss surrounds bog bridging on Isle au Haut's lightly used Bowditch Trail (Hike 36).*

ABOUT THE AUTHOR

Jeffrey Romano has been hiking throughout New England for more than forty years. Born in Connecticut, Jeff grew up in southern New Hampshire exploring the White Mountains and other New England trails with his family. He earned a BA in politics from Saint Anslem College and a JD from Vermont Law School and has worked for various nonprofit organizations over the past three decades. Jeff currently manages public policy activities for Maine Coast Heritage Trust, a statewide land trust that conserves properties around Acadia National Park and along the rest of Maine's unique coast.

When not advocating for land conservation in the Maine State House, he often explores the outdoors of New England with his family and dreams about future adventures in Italia—*Forza Azzurri!* An avid birdwatcher, Jeff lives in Hallowell, Maine, with his wife, Maria, and their children, Sabrina and Anthony. He is also the author of *Best Loop Hikes: New Hampshire's White Mountains to the Maine Coast*, *100 Classic Hikes in New England*, and *Day Hiking: New England*—all three published by Mountaineers Books.